50 Years of Singapore-Europe Relations

Celebrating Singapore's Connections with Europe

World Scientific Series on Singapore's 50 Years of Nation-Building

Published

50 Years of Social Issues in Singapore
 edited by David Chan (Singapore Management University, Singapore)

Our Lives to Live: Putting a Woman's Face to Change in Singapore
 edited by Kanwaljit Soin and Margaret Thomas

50 Years of Singapore–Europe Relations: Celebrating Singapore's Connections with Europe
 edited by Yeo Lay Hwee (EU Centre, Singapore) and Barnard Turner (National University of Singapore, Singapore)

Forthcoming

Food, Foodways and Foodscapes: Culture, Community and Consumption in Post-Colonial Singapore
 edited by Lily Kong and Vineeta Sinha (National University of Singapore, Singapore)

50 Years of Chinese Community in Singapore
 edited by Pang Cheng Lian (Former Singapore's Ambassador to Switzerland and Italy)

50 Years of Engineering in Singapore
 edited by Cham Tao Soon (Emeritus President, Nanyang Technological University, Singapore)

50 Years of Environment: Singapore's Journey Towards Environmental Sustainability
 edited by Tan Yong Soon (Former Permanent Secretary of the Ministry of the Environment and Water Resources, Singapore & Former Permanent Secretary in the National Climate Change Secretariat in the Prime Minister's Office, Singapore)

50 Years of Eurasian Community
 edited by Timothy James De Souza (The Eurasian Association, Singapore)

Singapore's Health Care System: What 50 Years Have Achieved
 by K. Satkunanantham (National University Health System, Singapore) and Lee Chien Earn (Changi General Hospital, Singapore)

50 Years of Indian Community
 edited by Gopinath Pillai (Ministry of Foreign Affairs, Singapore)

50 Years of Malay-Muslim Community
 edited by Zainul Abidin Rasheed (Former President, Singapore Islamic Religious Council, Singapore)

(Continued at end of book)

World Scientific Series on
Singapore's 50 Years of Nation-Building

50 YEARS OF SINGAPORE-EUROPE RELATIONS

Celebrating Singapore's Connections with Europe

Editors

Yeo Lay Hwee
European Union (EU) Centre, Singapore

Barnard Turner
National University of Singapore, Singapore

Published by

World Scientific Publishing Co. Pte. Ltd.
5 Toh Tuck Link, Singapore 596224
USA office: 27 Warren Street, Suite 401-402, Hackensack, NJ 07601
UK office: 57 Shelton Street, Covent Garden, London WC2H 9HE

Library of Congress Cataloging-in-Publication Data
50 years of Singapore-Europe relations : celebrating Singapore's connections with Europe / edited by: Lay Hwee Yeo (EU Centre, Singapore), Barnard Turner (NUS, Singapore).
   pages cm. -- (World Scientific series on Singapore's 50 years of nation-building)
   Includes bibliographical references.
   ISBN 978-9814675550 -- ISBN 978-9814675567 (pbk)
   1. Europe--Relations--Singapore. 2. Singapore--Relations--Europe. 3. European Union countries--Relations--Singapore. 4. Singapore--Relations--European Union countries. I. Yeo, Lay Hwee, editor of compilation. II. Turner, Barnard, editor of compilation. III. Title: Fifty years of Singapore-Europe relations.
   D1065.S55A3 2015
   303.48'2595704--dc23

2015018718

British Library Cataloguing-in-Publication Data
A catalogue record for this book is available from the British Library.

Copyright © 2015 by World Scientific Publishing Co. Pte. Ltd.

All rights reserved. This book, or parts thereof, may not be reproduced in any form or by any means, electronic or mechanical, including photocopying, recording or any information storage and retrieval system now known or to be invented, without written permission from the publisher.

For photocopying of material in this volume, please pay a copying fee through the Copyright Clearance Center, Inc., 222 Rosewood Drive, Danvers, MA 01923, USA. In this case permission to photocopy is not required from the publisher.

In-house Editor: Li Hongyan

Typeset by Stallion Press
Email: enquiries@stallionpress.com

Printed in Singapore by Mainland Press Pte Ltd.

Contents

Introduction: Celebrating Singapore's Connections
with Europe — 50 Years and More　　　　　　　　　　　　　1
Yeo Lay Hwee

Section 1: Connections and Reflections — Multi-dimensional Facets of Singapore-Europe Relations　　　5

1. Singapore and Europe: 50 Years of Relations　　　7
   K. Shanmugam

2. Europe's Contribution to Singapore's Contemporary Culture　　　10
   Michael Pulch

3. Reflecting on Singapore's Contributions to Europe　　　15
   Yeo Lay Hwee

4. 1965 and 2015, Europe and Singapore: Some Changes and
   Constants in a Cultural Geography Perspective　　　22
   Barnard Turner

5. Debunking Some "Euromyths" — Understanding the
   European Union (EU) and Its Connections to Singapore　　　29
   Loke Hoe Yeong

6. The Asia-Europe Meeting (ASEM):
   A Bridge between East and West　　　34
   Goh Chok Tong

7. Singapore and the Asia Europe Foundation (ASEF)　　　38
   Tommy Koh and Peggy Kek

8. Singapore, Germany and the European Union — Political Dialogue for Closer Cooperation and Mutual Understanding 43
Wilhelm Hofmeister

Section 2: Enduring Bilateral Ties 49

9. Belgians in Singapore: Helping to Write the City-State's (Hi)story 51
Gerard Cockx

10. The Mermaid and the Merlion — 50 Years with Denmark and Singapore 56
Written by Mathilde Moyell Juul
(commissioned by the Royal Danish Embassy)

11. Preserving the Excellent Connection between Finland and Singapore through the Young Generation 61
Tuukka Väisänen

12. Cultural and Scientific Cooperation between Italy and Singapore 65
Contribution from the Embassy of Italy and Italian Cultural Institute

13. Singapore and Luxembourg: Small Partners, Big Visions! 68
Contribution from the Luxembourg Embassy

14. Singapore and the Netherlands: Building the Future Together 71
Katrijn de Ronde, Embassy of the Kingdom of the Netherlands

15. Polish People in Singapore: The Foundation of Strong Singapore-Poland Relations 77
Zenon Kosiniak-Kamysz and Katarzyna Kryczka

16. Singapore and Slovakia — Friendly Countries with a Strong Story 82
Michal Slivovič

Section 3: From Commerce and Industry to Education and Science 87

17. From Central Europe to Singapore: Bata and Baťa 89
Tomáš Smetánka

18. From Palm Oil to Consumer Goods' Giant 94
Benjamin Felix van Roij

19. Jebsen & Jessen (SEA) — A Singapore Story with
    European Roots 99
    Benjamin Felix van Roij

20. Siemens in Singapore — Building Partnerships 104
    Contribution from Siemens and Excel Marco

21. Science and Research Collaboration between Singapore
    and Europe 108
    Bertil Andersson and Tony Mayer

22. Engineering the Future: Academic Excellence between
    Germany and Singapore 114
    Contribution from TUM Asia (Technische Universität München Asia)

23. Irish Connections — Ireland's Intrepid Educationalists in Singapore 120
    Rosemary Lim

24. NUS' Connections with Europe: Our Students' Experience with
    European Partners 126
    Anne Pakir

Section 4: People Matter(s) 137

25. Brother Joseph McNally: Son of Ballintubber, Ireland
    and Singapore 139
    Molly Hennigan and Cheryl Julia Lee

26. Dr. Albert Winsemius: A Dutchman among Singapore's Pioneers 144
    Benjamin Felix van Roij

27. The Polish Professor Who "Maps our Brains" —
    Prof. Dr. Wieslaw L. Nowiński 150
    Charles Chia

28. Art and Science in Singapore in the Last 15 Years —
    A Personal Journey and Reflection 154
    Isabelle Desjeux

29. Beppe De Vito — The Italian Restaurateur 158
    Charles Chia

30. From Croatia to Singapore: Marko Kraljević's Journey 164
    Dexter Lee

Celebrating Singapore's Connections with Europe — 50 Years and More

Yeo Lay Hwee

Introduction

Being open, being connected and being forward-looking — these are traits that have served Singapore well. Singapore profits from its openness and proactive diplomacy in seeking connections with the outside world. As we reach our 50th birthday, we not only celebrate the journey Singaporeans have taken together to come this far, but should also honour and celebrate with our friends from around the globe: The countries that have established close diplomatic ties and built enduring partnerships, the companies and corporations that invested in Singapore and stayed despite uncertainties, those that came later and built on the success of Singapore, and the peoples around the world that have contributed in their own way to the development of a dynamic and diverse Singapore.

This book is dedicated to celebrating the rich, diverse, and wide-ranging ties that bind Singapore and Europe: from the official relations established over the years with many European countries, to the corporations and peoples who have come to our shores and become very much part of our economic and social landscapes. These burgeoning ties and connections have made Singaporean society richer in all aspects — not just materially, but culturally and in all dimensions.

As we celebrate our 50 years of independence, we remember and honour people like Dr. Albert Winsemius, an important figure in Singapore's industrialisation path and economic development and Brother Joseph McNally who was committed to Singapore and left behind a legacy in arts and arts education. We appreciate scientists like Dr. Wieslaw Nowinski who came and contributed to the nation's efforts to move towards a knowledge-based economy and extend our welcome to chef Beppe de Vito and football player and coach, Marko Kraljević, who each play a part in shaping respectively the dining and sporting scenes in Singapore.

This book is divided broadly into four sections — the first comprises a series of essays and articles that examine the overall connections between Singapore and Europe, the multilateral aspect of our partnership, the mutual learning that takes place and reflect on some of the changes and constants in Europe and Singapore from 1965 to 2015. Minister K. Shanmugam's article looks at how the Singapore-Europe relationship has blossomed and how the recently concluded EU-Singapore Free Trade Agreement (EUSFTA) and the EU-Singapore Partnership and Cooperation Agreement would further strengthen the links between Singapore, Southeast Asia and Europe. Ambassador Pulch's article also affirms the mutual benefits that the EUSFTA will bring to this partnership, but at the same time, also explores the wider contribution that Europe has made to Singapore's society. Dr. Yeo Lay Hwee's article in return looks at the contributions that Singapore has made to Europe, and wishes that more mutual learning will take place between Singaporeans and Europeans. Dr. Barnard Turner's reflective essay takes a cultural geography perspective and traces some of the iconic events that took place from 1965–2015 in Europe and Southeast Asia. While Europe as a geographic and cultural entity is quite familiar to Singaporeans, the European Union as a political entity is often misunderstood. Loke Hoe Yeong's article examines some of these common (mis)perceptions and tried to debunk some of these "euromyths" and put them in perspective.

Singapore's role to go beyond the bilateral and connect Europe to the broader East Asian region and build a bridge between East and West is explored in ESM Goh Chok Tong's essay on the Asia-Europe Meeting (ASEM). The support given by the Singapore government to establish the Asia-Europe Foundation (ASEF) is further testimony of Singapore's role, and the article by Ambassador Tommy Koh and Peggy Kek tells the story of the earlier days of ASEF. While ASEF has been instrumental in bringing about greater connections between Asia and Europe through its activities promoting people-to-people ties, intellectual and cultural exchanges, the Konrad-Adenauer-Stiftung (KAS), a German political foundation, has also been active in Southeast Asia in promoting political dialogue for closer cooperation and mutual understanding.

The second section consists of articles and essays that explore the partnership and the interactions between Singapore and several European countries. Ambassador Gerard Cockx has penned an article that celebrates the contributions of Belgians in Singapore — from history to education, from industry to arts, and not forgetting the culinary scene. The Danes trace their first contact with Singapore back to 1845, and have looked with wonder on the growing ties and the mutual learning that will further strengthen the relationship between Singapore and

Denmark in the future. From the eyes of a young Finnish PhD student, the ties between Finland and Singapore can be further enhanced through educational and entrepreneurial exchanges. Italy prides itself for the work done by the Italian Cultural Institute in bringing about noteworthy exchanges with Singapore in the fields of Art, Music, Education and Science.

A kindred spirit exists between Singapore and Luxembourg as both are conscious of their relative "smallness" and have thus developed an essentially international outlook. The Netherlands' strong ties with Singapore started with Van Kleef, Philips and Winsemius, and since then the two countries have been forging ahead to build the future together. Poland established official diplomatic ties with Singapore in 1969, but it was not until the 1990s that the relationship intensified. Yet, at a different level, Poles have been making a mark in this Little Red Dot, from Joseph Conrad to Czeslaw Stania, Olszewski to Nowinski. Slovakia, a relatively young nation, at first glance may not seem to have much in common with Singapore. Yet, both offer compelling stories of how vision and gumption of its leaders and peoples have made them well-functioning, successful nations.

The third section of the book celebrates the wide ranging connections and collaborations in the areas of commerce, education, science and research. The story of Bata (the shop) and Baťa (its founder) is a fascinating account of the history of the shoe company in Singapore that is sure to tug at the hearts of those Singaporeans who grew up remembering the slogan "First to Bata then to school". The company Unilever may not be a "household" name, yet it would be no exaggeration to claim that one of its products, from soap, shampoo to food and beverages, can be found in all Singaporean homes. The story of Jebsen & Jessen (SEA) with its headquarters in Singapore, and its Chairman, Heinrich Jessen, a naturalised Singaporean of Danish descent, is an interesting story of a European family business with strong Asian roots. Siemens, in Singapore since 1908, prides itself on efforts in building strong partnerships with local companies. To date, Siemens has over 35 partnerships in Singapore and its quality partnership with Excel Marco is one of them.

In the article on Science and Research collaboration between Singapore and Europe, Professor Bertil Andersson and Tony Mayer look at the rapid changes taking place in the science and research landscape and laud the efforts by the Singapore government to build a knowledge-based economy by investing heavily in science, research and innovation. A good example of the intensifying cooperation between Singapore and several European countries in science and technology and in technical education is Singapore's invitation to the Technical University of Munich (TUM) to set up a campus in Singapore. TUM Asia is an example of how far education excellence has taken root. This is certainly very different from the colonial days when schools were established by the missionaries. Rosemary Lim's article explores Irish connections to Singapore through the intrepid educationalists — the

Irish teaching missionaries who first set foot in Singapore in 1852. While Irish missionaries have contributed to the education of Singaporeans for generations, the National University of Singapore (NUS) in helping to build the nation's capital has increasingly emphasised the importance of students being global minded and culturally sensitive. The student exchange programme and collaborations with European universities have become an important part of NUS strategy to offer high value education to its students.

The final section of the book contains essays about and interviews with Europeans who have made Singapore home — physically or in spirit. Brother Joseph McNally, son of Ballintubber, Ireland and Singapore, came to Singapore in 1946 and contributed to Singapore's education and arts scene for over 40 years until his passing in 2002. Dr. Albert Winsemius, an important economic advisor to the Singapore government, was described in a newspaper headline as "the Dutchman behind Singapore Inc." Wieslaw L. Nowinski, the Polish professor who came to Singapore in 1991, through his brain mapping has helped put Singapore on the global map. Isabelle Desjeux, who came to Singapore in 1999 as a biologist, gives her own reflection in the essay on her decision to cross frontiers to venture into the arts, and then to use her background as both a scientist and artist to break down boundaries and embrace differences. In the interview with Italian restaurateur Beppe de Vito, he recounts his journey into the food and beverage business in Singapore, and the changes in the dining scene, and hopes for the emergence of a more matured and self-assured Singapore. Who would have known that in the 2014 season of the S-League, there were some 20 Europeans contributing to local football in different capacities? And one of them is Marko Kraljević, football coach of S-League Club Balestier Khalsa. His story of dreams, hard work and discipline is something that we hope Singaporeans can relate to.

We hope that this rich collection of essays and articles celebrating the different dimensions of Singapore-Europe connections will not only be an interesting read, but will serve as a reminder that success of a society comes from collaboration and not just competition. As Singapore ponders its next 50 years, let us continue to strengthen this culture of openness, acceptance of diversities, and growing our links and connections with the outside world.

Section 1

Connections and Reflections — Multi-dimensional Facets of Singapore-Europe Relations

Singapore and Europe: 50 Years of Relations

K. Shanmugam

2015 marks the 50th year of Singapore's independence. This is a chance to reflect on how far we have come as a nation since independence was suddenly thrust upon us in 1965. Singapore had to contend with high unemployment, low education levels, a shortage of housing and poor living standards. We needed to build a military and diplomatic service from scratch, and above all foster a new national identity. Against the odds, Singapore managed to not only survive but prosper, lifting itself from third world to first. We now consistently rank as one of the most liveable places in the world; the unemployment rate has not exceeded 6% for over 25 years (it currently stands at 2%); more than 90% of Singaporeans own their homes; and half of our labour force has tertiary education. A Singaporean born today can expect to live to 82, 16 more years than the average life expectancy of a citizen born five decades ago.

As a small country, Singapore has always understood the importance of international connections and an open economy. Since the founding of modern Singapore, usually dated to Sir Stamford Raffles' establishment of a trading post on our island in 1819, Singapore has served as a major hub connecting Asia and Europe. Landmarks in Singapore such as Waterloo Street and the Fullerton Hotel bear witness to these early links. Many European firms, including Siemens and Shell, have long histories in Singapore spanning more than a century. Their enduring presence is a reminder of the synergistic nature of Singapore-Europe relations. Europe has also been instrumental to Singapore's post-independence success. Denmark, France, Germany, Italy, the Netherlands and the UK were among the first to recognise Singapore as a sovereign state. Our navy's first gunboats were jointly produced by German and British firms, while our first military pilots were trained in the UK. On the economic front, the late Dutch economist Dr. Albert Winsemius was a key architect of our export-driven development strategy.

The Singapore-Europe relationship has blossomed into a deep and comprehensive partnership that is based on enduring mutual interests. At the political level, Singaporean and European leaders regularly exchange visits. At the people-to-people level, over 1.5 million Europeans visited Singapore in 2013. The 60,000-strong European community in Singapore has greatly enriched our society. As for economic links, the EU is the largest investor in Singapore, while Singapore is the EU's second-largest Asian investor. Bilateral trade amounts to over €60 billion per year. Defence relations remain strong, with equipment purchases flowing in both directions. Cultural ties are similarly flourishing — 2015 will see a number of cultural events held in various European cities to commemorate the 50th anniversary of Singapore's independence. These include the Singapore Festival in France 2015 and Singapore's return to the Venice Biennale.

The Singapore-Europe relationship will undoubtedly continue to evolve, in no small part due to the important changes taking place in the world today. Propelled by the rapid growth of emerging economies such as China, India, Indonesia and Vietnam, the 21st century will make the Asia-Pacific a dynamic region. The 21 Asia-Pacific Economic Cooperation (APEC) economies represent 55% of the world's GDP and conduct 44% of its trade. The Asian Development Bank further predicts that, by 2050, Asia could account for more than half of global GDP, trade and investment. The Association of Southeast Asian Nations (ASEAN), comprising 10 Southeast Asian countries (including Singapore), lies at the heart of the dynamic Asia-Pacific region. In 2015, the ASEAN countries are due to form an ASEAN Economic Community, a single market and production base with 600 million consumers and a strong economic outlook. The ASEAN economy will be one of the top 10 economies in the world today.

Europe's long-term prosperity will be enhanced if it fully taps into the economic vibrancy of ASEAN. The EU is in a good position to step up its engagement through fora such as the ASEAN-EU Dialogue Partnership, the ASEAN Regional Forum, and the Asia-Europe Meeting. I welcome the EU's decision to appoint its first dedicated Ambassador to ASEAN. The EU has also embarked on bilateral trade negotiations with Singapore, Vietnam, Malaysia and Thailand, all of which will serve as building blocks for deeper region-to-region economic collaboration. Against this backdrop, the recently-concluded EU-Singapore Free Trade Agreement (EUSFTA) and EU-Singapore Partnership and Cooperation Agreement (ESPCA) take on special significance.

The EUSFTA will bring substantial benefits to both parties. The EU enjoys a €11.6 billion trade surplus with Singapore, and will benefit from the tariff-free access and recognition of Geographical Indications. European companies in Singapore, which currently number 10,400, will benefit from ASEAN cumulation and Singapore's network of FTAs to increase their exports to rapidly growing markets. It is estimated that the EUSFTA will boost EU exports to Singapore by €1.4 billion and EU real GDP by €550 million over 10 years.[1] The EUSFTA will also stimulate green growth by removing obstacles to trade and investment in environmentally friendly technologies. Strategically, the EUSFTA — the EU's first such agreement with a Southeast Asian country — will enhance the EU's engagement of Asia, and serve as a springboard to an eventual EU-ASEAN FTA. It is therefore vital that the EU ratifies the EUSFTA as soon as possible and sends a strong signal that Europe remains open for business. Such bilateral initiatives, along with mooted region-to-region agreements like the EU-ASEAN Comprehensive Air Transport Agreement, will augment connections, boost growth and create jobs to the benefit of the EU's and ASEAN's 1.1 billion citizens.

Even as we celebrate Singapore's 50th birthday, we are not resting on our laurels; we are now looking forward to the next 50 years. We are investing in our people by providing rigorous and broad-based education up to the university level and implementing bold social policies. In particular, we are focussing extensively on ensuring that our young people can access skills-based education, and not just focus on getting a university degree, so that they can compete in the modern world economy. We are also enhancing our physical infrastructure by doubling our train network and expanding our airport. In the next 50 years, we hope to become an exceptional global city with a thriving economy, where Singaporeans have good jobs whilst enjoying a high-quality life with families and friends. In realising this vision, we remain committed to the values that have underpinned our success — incorruptibility, meritocracy, multiculturalism, democracy and openness to the world — values that Europe shares. I am confident that the EU will continue to make positive contributions to the success and prosperity of Singapore and the region.

· · · · ·

This article was originally published in New Europe's January 2015 publication, "Our World in 2015".

K. Shanmugam is Minister for Foreign Affairs and Minister for Law, Singapore.

---

[1] Figures are from "The economic impact of the EU-Singapore Free Trade Agreement," an analysis prepared by the European Commission's Director-General for Trade, published in September 2013.

Europe's Contribution to Singapore's Contemporary Culture

Michael Pulch

When Singapore officially celebrates its 50 years of independence on 9 August 2015, it can look back to one of Asia's most successful stories of economic development. Due to its good governance, its forward-looking, often truly visionary policies and its well-educated, hardworking citizens, Singapore has become, in just five decades, the vibrant cosmopolitan city that it is today. The "Lion City" is admired around the world for this unprecedented achievement.

Throughout its history, Singapore has been at the crossroads of many cultural influences. Here the Malay, Chinese, Indian and European cultures, languages, arts and crafts met, mixed and mingled to create the unique blend of present day Singapore. In many ways Singapore represents the best of all worlds, as demonstrated by its indigenous, diverse cuisine which uses elements of other culinary traditions with a local twist.

Europe, together with its people, has always been an important and distinctive ingredient of the Singaporean flavour. The enriching interaction between Singapore and Europe has contributed to its economic success, cultural diversity and modern lifestyle.

Singapore's independence has broadened and intensified this cross-fertilisation. In that regard, the steadily increasing commercial ties have played an important role. Today, more than 10,000 European companies are registered here, three times the number of the next major economic player. No other economic partner has invested more in Singapore than the European Union and vice versa; indeed, Singapore has become the EU's 5th largest investor outside of Europe. This is a remarkable accomplishment that shows confidence in the future development of both economies. Trade statistics show the EU to be amongst the top 3 trading partners in goods and latest available figures suggest that if trade in goods and services are taken together, the EU might even be the most important commercial relationship for Singapore.

These are significant markers for the EU's engagement here. Moreover, a number of initiatives have been launched recently to enhance prospects for the future. A Free Trade Agreement, now finally concluded, contains the most advanced provisions in any such agreement negotiated by the EU to date. A new programme for European small and medium-sized enterprises, "Business Avenues to Southeast Asia", launched here in October 2014, will bring more than 1,000 European SMEs to Singapore and other ASEAN countries. Work has also started on the critically important air services sector, following the first EU-ASEAN aviation summit held during Singapore's aviation week in February 2014.

These form but one aspect of the long-standing economic, political and cultural relationship that binds together Europe and Southeast Asia. When Singapore commemorates its 50th anniversary, it can celebrate an enormously successful period of its much longer history. Throughout that history many European countries played their part in creating the global hub that Singapore has become today, foremost in that regard, the United Kingdom. Throughout the centuries, others contributed as well: the Portuguese, Spanish, Dutch and French to name a few prominent seafarer nations, developed commercial and cultural ties with Singapore and South East Asia. However, it was a Belgian, to be precise a Flemish trader from Bruges named Jacques de Coutre, who wrote the first European travel accounts in which he mentioned a place called "Singapura" and described the strategic location of this island. In 2013, the National University of Singapore Press published a book, edited by the Academic Convenor of its European Studies Programme, Peter Borschberg, describing de Coutre's adventures sailing under the Portuguese flag in the early 17th century. His memoirs and memorials of security, trade and society in Southeast Asia, handwritten in Spanish and kept in the National Library in Madrid, present a lively picture of a period that in many ways laid the foundation for the vast trading networks across the Indian Ocean and the South China Sea that continue to link Europe and Southeast Asia. It was through these trading routes, with the establishment of the British port in Singapore at its centre that cultural exchange flourished.

The European cultural footprint has become a distinctive feature of modern Singapore, setting the city-state apart from other major ports and capitals in the region. This interaction further enhances the trade and commercial relationship and encompasses Singapore's architectural development, academic institutions and education, the arts scene, lifestyle, fashion and entertainment.

One of Singapore's signature traits is its unique blend of architecture. It successfully combines the glitzy new buildings in the financial district with its architectural heritage, the famous English-style "black and white houses" and the magnificent colonial buildings, including the impressive National Museum, the newly renovated Victoria Hall and the former City Hall that will soon host the National Art Gallery. During its initial years after independence the government invited some of the best city planners from around the world to Singapore. Part of the United Nations team of consultants was a Polish architect, Krystyn Olszewski, from Warsaw University who was appointed chief designer of Singapore's Comprehensive Long-Term Concept Plan. This plan envisaged some of the fundamental infrastructural developments that define the layout of Singapore today. The proposals foresaw a city built on connectivity, in particular a rail-based mass transport system, and the building of a new airport, the much admired Changi Airport, at its present location.

The iconic landmark, Marina Bay Sands, was built later on reclaimed land together with "Gardens by the Bay" to become a relatively new feature of Singapore's urban development that attracts Singaporean citizens and tourists alike. Many of the reclamation works were undertaken in cooperation with Dutch and Belgian companies that offered their expertise in this area, as well as in water protection. This is based on longstanding bilateral partnerships on water management that exist with these two countries and also with Denmark.

Singapore's reputation as one of Asia's up and coming academic centres of excellence is built on its first-rate choice of local and international schools and its range of highly regarded universities. One of the contributing factors to their success has always been a close cooperation with European academic institutions from across the continent and a constant exchange of professors and researchers. The annual EU Education Fair presents opportunities for Singaporean students to broaden their experience by undertaking part of their studies in Europe. These people-to-people contacts continue to promote a strong relationship, fostered by generations of Singaporeans who spent time in the United Kingdom and other European countries during their formative years and returned home with fond memories of student life in cosmopolitan cities or picturesque university towns. Moreover, the Government has taken an active interest in promoting apprenticeships and vocational training for young Singaporeans, following the examples of Scandinavian countries, Austria and Germany.

European art and culture were present in Singapore right from the beginning of its rise as a leading port, as witnessed by a number of earlier buildings devoted to stage concerts or theatre plays. There are some fascinating stories, often long forgotten, of pioneers who brought new art forms to Singapore. One of them was the French entrepreneur, Paul Picard, who in 1904 opened Singapore's first enclosed cinema, the "Paris Cinematograph", in the Malay Theatre located at 320 Victoria Street. Before this, early cinema screenings were held in tents in open spaces along Victoria Street or at the foot of Fort Canning Hill. The earliest silent movies depicted the Russo-Japanese war of that same year, comedy and sports. Today, Singapore has emerged as an entertainment centre on the global scene, offering a rich programme of local and international performances in all art forms from classical music concerts of renowned European composers, theatre performances that include annual open air Shakespeare performances to painting exhibitions in cooperation with leading European museums. Since 1904, movies have maintained their place as an important part of Singapore's cultural calendar, as seen by Singapore's own longstanding film festival. Apart from a number of national film weeks organised by its member states, the EU is proud to run the oldest foreign film festival in Singapore, which in 2015 celebrates its 25th anniversary. Throughout these years, the European Union Film Festival (EUFF) has offered Singaporeans a glimpse at the different facets of European movies varying from art house films to Oscar winning productions.

Singapore's own arts scene has always taken its inspiration from the various cultural influences that form the basis of its constituting communities. This is exemplified in the story of the painter Lee Man Fong, one of the eight Singaporean pioneer artists honoured in a video by the then Ministry of Community Development. Born in Guangdong province, raised in Singapore and Indonesia where he started his career, he received his formal art training on a scholarship in the Netherlands and held his first solo exhibitions there. During his last 20 years of work in Singapore until his death in 1988, his mastery at blending Eastern and Western influences in oil painting made him one of the most recognised artists here, with one of his paintings "Bali Life" becoming the most expensive Southeast Asian artwork on auction to date.

One aspect of European influence on lifestyle in Singapore is how much its citizens are into European, to be precise classical British, sports activities, be it tennis, cricket, golf or football. The city offers a variety of sports facilities unparalleled in other regional capitals. Amateur football matches and cricket games in the afternoon are a regular sight on the Padang located right in the city centre, a potential distraction from work, as they occur in full view of the EU Delegation's office windows. Few other sports events capture public interest as much as the results of the English Premier League and the final rounds of the annual European Champions League. Although the "The Lions" may not always live up to the expectation of its supporters, one of Singapore's most successful and legendary football players, Fandi Ahmad, became the first Singaporean to join a first league team in Europe, FC Groningen, and to score a goal in a European Cup competition — against Inter Milan. There are hopes that more Singaporeans can follow in his footsteps, especially as football powerhouse Real Madrid has opened one of its global Technical Academies here.

Of course, one of the easiest predictions to be made during the annual F1 race in Singapore, which quickly established itself as one of the F1 signature racing courses, is to forecast that a European driver will win, which has been the case ever since Singapore became part of the circuit.

Arguably there is no better place in this part of the world than Singapore to check out, compare and buy European fashion and lifestyle products. Every single European brand, so it seems, has established its own outlet in the city. One of the attractions for the millions of visitors to Singapore, including large numbers of European citizens, is in fact to go on a shopping spree for the latest European brands. High class fashion design weeks or exhibitions are regularly organised by fairs from European countries, notably the French, Italian and Spanish. Others obviously make their mark as well: for example, last year brought the biggest ever diamond trade show from Antwerp to Singapore. Fashion does not end there; few other places in the world see such a variety of European luxury cars on its streets.

An important part of Singaporean lifestyle centres on food in all its forms: food products, recipes, restaurants and different cuisines. Europe makes its contribution to the fascinating mix of tastes available locally. Not only are Italian and French restaurants amongst the most frequented here, the bar scene is dominated by English and Irish pubs and the occasional German-style "Brauhaus". Refined agricultural products and beverages are readily available all year round for the tens of thousands of resident European expatriates as well as for Singaporeans who have acquired a taste for the various specialities originating from across Europe. For consumers the EU-Singapore Free Trade Agreement will be good news: once implemented it will result in enhanced choice, lowered prices and increased consumer protection through labelling requirements. They can be sure then that if they choose "Prosciutto di Parma", Greek "feta" cheese and Hungarian "Tokaj" wine for instance, these delicacies are indeed produced there, as these geographical indications will be protected henceforth.

There are of course many more facets of European culture to be found in Singapore that have contributed to its unique charm. Hopefully, the gorgeous Botanic Gardens will receive the approval to join the list of world cultural heritage sites during this Jubilee year. The 50th anniversary will be an opportunity to look back at the many achievements of Singapore and its people. It will also present the country's distinctive blend of cultures that makes it one of the globe's most coveted places to live, work and visit. Europe can be proud to add its flavour to the Singapore hotpot, today and in the future. Cultural exchanges will always continue to flow in both directions and the Singapore Arts Festival to be held in France this year will be an occasion for Europeans to also get acquainted with the arts, music and dance from the "Lion City" and to savour its cuisine.

H.E. Dr. Michael Pulch is Ambassador and Head of the EU Delegation office in Singapore.

Reflecting on Singapore's Contributions to Europe

Yeo Lay Hwee

Introduction

My personal connections with Europe began in 1995 at a Japanese-American pub known as the *Cable Car*. This was where I met my Danish architect husband, Poul. I like to joke that we are both involved in building bridges — mine are imaginary and intellectual ones to bring about closer cooperation and connections between Asia and Europe, while he builds real bridges to bring about greater physical connectivity.

My professional connections with Europe also began in 1995, working at the Institute of Policy Studies where I was employed as a Research Associate. I was primarily involved as the Resource person for the Eminent Persons Group looking at revitalising ASEAN-EU partnership.

So, I have much to celebrate in my 20 years of connections with Europe.

Singapore's connections to Europe, of course, date much further back in time. Besides the fact that it was a former British colony, it was also a trading hub and an important port in the region since the 14th century. After its "discovery" by Stamford Raffles in 1819, its status as a free port attracted many traders from Asia and Europe to Singapore. Many European trading firms set up merchant houses in Singapore then.

Fast forward to 1965 with Singapore's independence achieved unexpectedly and with much trepidation. Being a small state and feeling vulnerable, Singapore was keenly aware of its limitations in material hard power and hence invested a lot in diplomacy. Singapore has since established diplomatic relations with 187 sovereign states and participates in all major multilateral forums and is a member of many international institutions.

Six European states — France, Denmark, Italy, Germany, United Kingdom and Netherlands — were among a dozen or so who established diplomatic ties with Singapore in 1965. Since then, Singapore has established ties with all 28 member states of the European Union (EU).[1] The Delegation of the European Union set up its office in Singapore in 2002 in recognition of the increasing ties, and at the end of 2012, the EU concluded negotiations for its first Free Trade Agreement (FTA) in Southeast Asia with Singapore.

The Multi-dimensional and Multi-layered Ties between Singapore and Europe

Reflecting on the last 50 years of Singapore's development, it has been remarkable that Singapore did not succumb to the post-colonial xenophobic nationalism that was prevalent in the 1960s, and had chosen an economic strategy that opened the door wide to foreign direct investments (FDI). Concerted efforts were also made to attract multinational corporations (MNCs) and foreign companies to set up shop in Singapore, many of them from Europe (from Unilever to Jebsen & Jessen, Shell to BP, Siemens to Rolls Royce, Philips to Electrolux). One could of course explain that since Singapore is just too small and without its own hinterland, it has no choice but to be open and to pursue an export-oriented strategy.

A European, Dutch economist Albert Winsemius, played an important part in formulating Singapore's economic development strategy. He was Singapore's long-term economic advisor from 1961 to 1984 and worked very closely with then Prime Minister, Lee Kuan Yew and then Deputy Prime Minister, Goh Keng Swee in "industrialising" Singapore and transforming Singapore from an entrepôt trade port into a manufacturing centre.

To complement the transfer of skills and technology, incentives were also provided for foreign firms to set up training centres in the 1960s and 1970s for Singapore workers, and this was later extended to cooperation with developed nations to establish technical training centres such as the German-Singapore Institute of Production Technology and the French-Singapore Institute for Electrotechnology.[2]

From these snapshots, one could say that Singapore's connections with Europe have been strong and the governments, companies and peoples of Europe have contributed in different ways to the development and transformation of Singapore.

---

[1] The 28 member states of the European Union are Austria, Belgium, Bulgaria, Croatia, Czech Republic, Denmark, Estonia, Finland, France, Germany, Greece, Hungary, Ireland, Italy, Latvia, Lithuania, Luxembourg, Malta, Netherlands, Poland, Portugal, Romania, Slovakia, Slovenia, Spain, Sweden and the UK.
[2] Gundy Cahyadi, et al., "Singapore's Economic Transformation," Global Urban Development's Singapore Metropolitan Economic Strategy Report, June 2004.

However, what about Singapore's contributions to the EU and Europe?

Singapore has often been said to "punch above its weight" in foreign policy and international relations. Its first generation diplomats, many of them "accidental" such as Professor Tommy Koh, have played an important role in the "internationalisation" of Singapore. Professor Koh, the consummate diplomat and negotiator, in particular, has been associated with various UN initiatives, being the President of the Third United Nations Conference on the Law of the Sea (1980–1982) which resulted in the United Nations Convention on the Law of the Sea (UNCLOS) III agreement. He also chaired the United Nations Conference on Environment and Development, also known as the Rio Summit in 1992. The 10-day meeting resulted in several important political declarations and legally binding agreements. However, lesser known perhaps but no less important, is his appointment as Special UN Envoy to the Baltic States in 1993.

The mission to the Baltics concerned the demand of Estonia, Latvia and Lithuania for the full withdrawal of Russian troops from their territories. These three Baltic States had had their independence restored in 1991 following the dissolution of the Soviet empire. Russia signed an agreement to recognise their independence that year. However, Russian troops remained in their territories as Russia struggled to manage the return of the Red Army from various former Soviet republics which had become independent. The successful mission by Tommy Koh resulted in a phased withdrawal of the troops. Assistance was also provided by Denmark, Norway and the US to help build housing for the returning troops and their families in Russia.[3]

The Baltic States have since made extraordinary improvement in their socioeconomic conditions. They became members of the North Atlantic Treaty Organization (NATO) and of the EU in 2004, and all three countries have also adopted the euro (Estonia in 2011, Latvia in 2014 and Lithuania in 2015) showing continued optimism in the currency despite the financial and debt crisis in Europe.

Singapore has also tried to serve as the interlocutor between the East and West. It contributed to the early 1990s debate on Asian values. The rationale for stirring up this debate was to respond to the triumphalism of the West in the early years of the end of the Cold War whilst preventing the beginning of another cold war between an emerging China and a triumphant America.[4]

---

[3] See Tommy Koh, *The Tommy Koh Reader: Favourite Essays and Lectures* (Singapore: World Scientific, 2013), 61–68.
[4] See Bilahari Kausikan's "The Idea of Asia," *The Straits Times*, 8 November 2014. Retrieved 19 February 2015 from http://www.straitstimes.com/news/opinion/more-opinion-stories/story/the-idea-asia-20141108.

In responding to the opening up of China and the increasing importance of East Asia to the global economy, Singapore way back in 1994 saw the need for greater engagement between East Asia and Europe. The idea presented was simple. The narrative was that Europe, East Asia and North America as the three engines of global growth need to understand each other more and work more closely. While transatlantic ties between Europe and America are strong because of historical and institutional reasons, and transpacific ties between East Asia and North America have been bolstered with the launch of Asia-Pacific Economic Cooperation (APEC), institutional ties between East Asia and Europe were relatively weak. To strengthen this third link, Singapore under then Prime Minister Goh Chok Tong went to Europe to canvass support for a leaders' summit between East Asian and European leaders. The Asia-Europe Meeting (ASEM) comprising ASEAN plus China, Japan and South Korea on the Asian side and the 15 EU member states and the Commission on the European side was launched in 1996.

ASEM was a symbol of Asia's and Europe's rediscovery of each other, and of the aspirations for stronger ties. Since then, the interdependence between Asia and Europe has deepened, ASEM has enlarged to 53 partners, and Singapore continues to advocate a pragmatic approach towards our bi-regional ties.

The initiative by Singapore to set up an Asia-Europe Foundation (ASEF) to complement the ASEM process is a sign of strong commitment from Singapore to help strengthen ties between Asia and Europe at the people-to-people level. ASEF, founded in 1997 and located in Singapore, is now the only "brick and mortar" institution of ASEM devoted to what the former President of the European Council, Herman van Rompuy called "the cross-fertilisation of ideas". Van Rompuy added that he had only praise of the vision of Goh Chok Tong that led to the launch of ASEM and ASEF two decades ago.[5]

The founding Executive Director of ASEF was Tommy Koh, and together with his team in ASEF he initiated a number of projects that brought together academics and researchers, artists, editors and journalists, teachers and students, and youths from Asia and Europe. As ASEF approaches its 20th anniversary in 2017 it can look back with satisfaction that it has succeeded in building many new bridges of understanding and friendship between Asia and Europe.

In contributing to the broader Asia-Europe relations, EU and Singapore ties have also grown in importance. The EU opened its Delegation office in 2002, and Singapore is the first Southeast Asian country to conclude a Free Trade Agreement (FTA) with the EU. The EU-Singapore FTA is the most comprehensive agreement

---

[5] Speech by Herman Van Rompuy, President of the European Council at the Schuman Lecture organised by the European Chamber of Commerce in Singapore.

that the EU has ever negotiated with a third country and will serve as a benchmark for other countries in the region as well as a stepping stone eventually for an EU-ASEAN FTA.

Singapore enjoys excellent bilateral ties not only with the UK for historical reasons, but with many other EU member states such as France, Germany, Ireland, the Netherlands, Sweden, to name a few. These ties are not only political and commercial but also in education exchanges, scientific and research collaboration, etc.

In many ways, Singapore served as an entry point, a gateway for many European companies into ASEAN. Singapore is host to over 10,000 European companies and more than 60,000 Europeans live and work in Singapore. Singapore's active role in ASEAN in the last two decades has also indirectly helped the EU to realise the strategic importance of ASEAN in the broader Asia-Pacific region. Though the EU and ASEAN had established a formal partnership since 1977, it has only been in the last few years that the EU has begun to place more emphasis on its engagement with ASEAN.

However, it is not only in trade that the EU and Singapore are natural partners. Singapore has, in the last two decades, with the setting up of the Singapore Cooperation Programme (SCP), actively sought to work with development agencies, banks and other developed countries in Europe to offer various training courses that can help build capacity and promote human resource development in the newer ASEAN member states such as Cambodia, Laos, Myanmar and Vietnam. For instance, Singapore is the first Southeast Asian country to work with the European Commission on a technical assistance programme for developing countries. The programme, which started in 2004, covered technical assistance in particular to Cambodia, Laos and Vietnam.

The opening of a European Union Centre in Singapore, the only such Centre in Southeast Asia, is another recognition by the EU of Singapore's important hub status in the region. In the call for proposals to set up an EU Centre in Singapore, the Commission noted that "EU's relations with Singapore are underpinned by very strong commercial ties" and that "Singapore acts as the hub for European business in the Asia-Pacific region". Furthermore, Singapore is also seen as an important education hub in Southeast Asia, and the Centre would therefore be "particularly well located to promote the policies and awareness of the EU".

Despite the big presence of European companies and Europeans in Singapore, there is certainly still a lack of awareness with regards to the functioning of the EU. The EU Centre tries to address this lack of awareness and understanding through its various outreach programmes and publications. The strong bilateral ties that Singapore enjoys with several EU member states sometimes obscure the importance of the EU. However, as Singapore begins to play an active role in ASEAN to promote closer regional cooperation, the EU is increasingly seen as a reference point for ASEAN as the latter seeks to achieve its goal of building an ASEAN Community by the end of 2015.

The EU is one of the most integrated economic blocs, with a single market of over 500 million consumers and citizens enjoying the four freedoms (free movement of goods, services, capital and people). While the EU's complex institutional structure and decision-making process make the EU democratic and resilient, it is also often associated with its inflexibility and inability to respond quickly to external events. Despite the current debt problems in the Eurozone, the anaemic growth figures and high unemployment, one must not forget that the EU has delivered on peace and reconciliation and has contributed to the economic reconstruction and increasing living standards of many European citizens for several decades.

While Singaporeans learn more about the multilevel governance and complex institutional structures in the EU, Europeans living in Singapore would hopefully come to appreciate the Singapore paradox — the rich but also rigid diversities, the economically affluent but at times seen as "politically impoverished" city-state.

Many Europeans look upon their stay in Singapore as a "training ground" for their "real entry" into other parts of Asia. Singapore is in Asia and very much part of Asia, and its primarily Asian population comprises people of Chinese, Indian and Malay background. Therefore Singapore is supposed to provide a flavour of what "Asia" is to Europeans, but not too much as to knock them out of their comfort zone. Its "traditional Asianness" is cushioned by its familiar "Western modernity" where everything works like clockwork.

In some way, Singapore, this westernised Asian city-state, is some sort of a paradox that hopefully helps to challenge the "either-or" binary mindset, and also the teleological belief in linear progress. We can be economically free but not so politically free, we have rule of law and good governance but not necessarily two-party or multiparty liberal democracy as understood by the west. For Europeans who live and work in Singapore, they too must also be amused by the paradoxical "can do, entrepreneurial" spirit of the country as a whole — when we see how much the country has achieved in five decades, but at the same time this prevailing perception that Singaporeans are *kiasu* and *kiasi* (essentially, afraid of losing out and of doing something wrong) and hence unwilling to take risks.

Living in Singapore could therefore lead Europeans to question many of the assumptions they have on culture and tradition, development and modernity.

Concluding Remarks

Singapore's connections with Europe go much further back beyond 50 years. Connections were of course very much coloured by its colonial ties with the UK. However, since its independence in 1965, Singapore has built up a wealth of connections and relations with Europe far beyond the UK. Through its diplomacy, its active engagement in global and regional affairs, Singapore has much to share with the European countries. Through its involvement in ASEAN and ASEM, it has also strengthened ties with the European Union and its member states. And through its openness in welcoming companies, corporations and talents to its shore, it provides a rich environment for mutual learning and growth between Singaporeans and Europeans.

References

Cahyadi, Gundy, et al. (2004). Singapore's Economic Transformation. Global Urban Development's Singapore Metropolitan Economic Strategy Report, June 2004. Retrieved 3 March 2015 from http://www.globalurban.org/GUD%20Singapore%20MES%20Report.pdf.

Kausikan, Bilahari. (2014, November 8). The Idea of Asia. The Straits Times. Retrieved 19 February 2015 from http://www.straitstimes.com/news/opinion/more-opinion-stories/story/the-idea-asia-20141108.

Koh, Tommy. (2013). The Tommy Koh Reader: Favourite Essays and Lectures. Singapore: World Scientific Publisher.

. . . . .

This article was originally published in NUSS Commentary "Singapore@50: Reflections and Observations", April 2015.

Dr. Yeo Lay Hwee is Director of the EU Centre, Senior Research Fellow at the Singapore Institute of International Affairs and Adjunct Fellow at the S. Rajaratnam School of International Studies. Her research expertise is in the area of comparative regional integration, and on ASEAN-EU and Asia-Europe relations.

1965 and 2015, Europe and Singapore: Some Changes and Constants in a Cultural Geography Perspective

Barnard Turner

The past half century has of course seen some remarkable changes, a lengthy process of consolidation and healing across both Europe and Southeast Asia (from World War II, the Cold War, conflicts of many varieties in Southeast Asia). The resolution and commitment to patch together a workable interdependent regional architecture in both regions (such as the EU and ASEAN), and between them, for example, the Asia-Europe Meeting (ASEM), are abiding achievements of the period, as is the rise to global prominence of Germany and Singapore, to name but two of the most outstanding examples from either region. This progress is still generally measured by GDP expansion: both the EU and the South East Asian economies concern themselves with competitiveness, a popular and much discussed index. In other indices, the Scandinavian and a patchwork of other temperate, even dour countries seem entrenched towards the top; Singapore seems increasingly prominent in such charts, and with its expanding infrastructure and healthcare facilities seems poised to rise even higher.

Asia has indubitably been on the rise over the past 50 years. In 1965, Tokyo became the first Asian city for two centuries or so to be the largest urban conglomerate (by population) in the world. 50 years later, around two-thirds of the top 20, and the first six, are Asian cities; New York, which was the largest city through half the previous century, is 8th, and, of European cities, London, which was largest for a century before that, is 30th, a long way behind Moscow and slightly below Paris. In a late 2014 speech at the European Chamber of Commerce in Singapore, then-EU [aka European] Council President Herman Van Rompuy called "the re-emergence of Asia one of the mega-trends shaping our world." In the 1960s of course, this rise was often seen elsewhere in terms of the domino theory, and the emergence something to be restrained by any means necessary. 50 years on, Van Rompuy gestured towards interdependence and a mutual reliance of one segment of Eurasia on another, "Asia, one of the locomotives of world growth, also depends to a large extent on an open European market to keep up this performance."

Such figures and traits have of course hardly gone unnoticed in Europe. In 1965, however, perceptions in the UK at least were that it might do well to detach itself from parts "east of Suez." While the London *Times* of 10 August 1965 led its second section of overseas news with the story of Singapore's separation from Malaysia and full independence, the lead story in the overseas news section as a whole, and taking up more space, was that of the jailing of a British pro-Nazi sympathiser in Germany. At the height of summer, the South African cricket team's defeat of England exceeded the coverage given to the Singapore story. Equal in importance for the London newspaper to the future of the Federation, of Singapore, and their relations with Indonesia, was the long-term "shifting" of UK bases, and the following page's editorial sounded a note that was not long after to be a reality that British commitments were so "burdensome and incalculable" that they could lead to the country being "drawn into involvements without limits in time and space." 50 years later, and 44 years after the base closures and the beginning of the defence commitments known as the Five Power Defence Arrangements, several periods of such unlimited involvement, most if not all "east of Suez," spring readily to mind. Indeed, an April 2013 Briefing Paper from the British Royal United Services Institute speculates about a "return east of Suez." But in 1965, Southeast Asia was distant, relatively unknown beyond a few persistent traits, in which echoes of Somerset Maugham's stories resonated with anxiety about conflict in "Indochina." In 1970, Agatha Christie's "extravaganza" *Passenger to Frankfurt* presented a present-day diplomat returning to London from "Malaya" (*sic*). Clearly, Christie was not up to date with events in Southeast Asia and referred to the constituent area by its by-then rather antiquated name.

In the 1960s, the "swinging Sixties," western Europe at least socially was the young-again region, and while the Cold War and the domino theory tempered sentiment a little, this, for most of the young generation in Europe at least, was nothing a good pop or rock concert couldn't cure, tinged with a little political activism which was to outpour, in a European context, in the famous interventions of Spring '68, notably in Paris, London and Prague, in which issues like the Vietnam War and opposition to prevailing political status quo were brought into the foreground. In March 1965, the first US combat troops arrived in Vietnam; in May, the first skateboarding championships were held (in California — where else?). One week after Singapore became a sovereign state, the Beatles played at the Shea Stadium; while the British began gradually closing bases east of Suez, the "British invasion" was beginning in North America. While both the US (e.g. the Los Angeles Watts

Riots ongoing as the Beatles played) and Singapore experienced riots with significant loss of life in the 1964–1969 period, and the crackdowns in eastern European cities (especially in Prague) were sometimes bloody, the protests in London and even Paris were relatively peaceful. In a famous 1968 song, Jagger/Richards mentioned a "sleepy London town" that was no place for a "street fighting man."

In the early through to the mid-1960s, Europe's problems seemed much closer to home, and much less intractable: an accommodation, uneasy though it was, with the Warsaw Pact countries seemed to be holding, even if unsettled by the Berlin Blockade, then the Wall, the Cuban Missile Crisis, and later on by "Eurocommunism." French President De Gaulle tried, successfully for a while, to ring-fence the incipient European "Community of the Six," at least from the west. 1965 was the year of the "empty chair" crisis at the EEC Commission, an expression (fortunately for only a few months) of de Gaulle's opposition to more supra-nationalism than intergovernmentalism in European affairs. But the irrepressible Jean Monnet was pressing ahead with more of the former: on 9 May 1965, the 15th anniversary of the Schuman Declaration, he had given a speech in Berlin in which he welcomed Britain if on Europe's terms, mentioned the necessity for a common European foreign policy and gestured towards a common European currency. Yet, ironically, the spirit of de Gaulle has lived on in spite or maybe as a consequence of the realisation of such plans, as such opposition became a hallmark of the EEC (now of course transformed into the EU) from the time that the UK eventually joined in 1973, the year that both Germanies became full members of the United Nations.

The European Commission's Annual Growth Survey 2015, published on 28 November 2014, notes that "persistent low growth, close to zero inflation and high unemployment has [*sic*] become a primary concern." How different from the picture in 1965, when Germany (lest we forget, BOTH halves) was doing well; West Germany was indeed in the world's top three trading nations, a position which the country as a whole has retained post-1990 even if several Asian nations have entered the top rankings. Even if inflation was then a concern, unemployment was not, at least not in terms to which the Union has become accustomed of late.

Increasingly, technology drives growth. Yet even the most ubiquitous of technological advances can be traced back to periods long before the lifetimes of their current users. Relatively recently, the IBM room-size computer morphed into the desktop, then into the laptop and the iPhone, but all such devices extend the telegraph and telephone, both of which antedate today's smart societies by two or more generations, the former by more than 150 years. Those satellite communications which make possible contemporary mobile communications (and of course SatNav, GPS, etc.) began in 1962, with the launch of the Telstar satellite commemorated in a still memorable hit of the year.

Mobility has of course been a hallmark of the past half century; nomadicity and hybridity have become familiar terms, reversing the stigmas of the vagabond, itinerant and creolised of earlier epochs. 50 years ago, some Singaporean students went to Europe (predominantly the UK, and with a notable percentage of medical students heading for the Republic of Ireland); indeed, in the preceding generations, both Tunku Abdul Rahman and Lee Kuan Yew had both attended Cambridge University. But few came from Europe to Singapore. Today, some 10% of NUS undergraduates are incoming exchange students and more than 14% or so undergraduates are foreigners pursuing longer-term courses here. In 1965, fewer Europeans came to Southeast Asia for a short-term, casual visit, or a holiday. A London-Singapore flight could cost half an average English annual wage, and would stop some four times en route, sometimes setting down in Baghdad or Tehran. At that time, and even only 40 years ago, it was scarcely feasible to travel between Europe and Southeast Asia without a close glance at some spots in between, some cities which may today figure highly on the travel advisory websites of Western embassies. Today, flights may stop in the Gulf, although this is more likely to be Dubai or Abu Dhabi than Bahrain, a more standard transit stop even a quarter century ago, and passengers in transit be amazed at the cross-section of humanity flowing through the airport whose variety and interconnectivity are little short of a *Star Wars* space station or what, conversely, Baghdad or Tehran may have been hundreds, even a few thousand, years ago. Yet this variety is in a sense delusory. Many of the passengers are part of contemporary cosmopolitan Africa-Eurasia, a vast mosaic which intersects here, as it has done for three thousand or more years. We are all human throughput in transit between destinations.

Stereotypes however unfortunately have a prolonged afterlife, "othering" takes places across a broad range of fronts, from the political (suppositions about a country's "interests"),[1] economic ("taking our jobs"), to individual stereotypes. A "native" Englishman may express amazement at a teenage neighbour, of Asian origin, who speaks — now the third generation in the English Midlands — with a broad Birmingham accent, and an Italian be intrigued if a foreigner can overcome "Starbucks vocabulary" in ordering a *stretto* (and remembers to ask for a receipt). A white European ("Caucasian" in the common typology) in Singapore is sometimes held in a certain wonderment if he can hold chopsticks proficiently, if he doesn't particularly mind durians or is not prone to alcoholic rage and foul language, as he is sometimes characterised by certain elements in the online community here in posts which would perhaps be moderated out in equivalent European media. Mindsets are slow to change, even if literally moving across

---

[1] Hedley Bull, *The Anarchical Society: A Study of Order in World Politics*. 4th ed. (New York: Columbia University Press, 1977/2002), 63.

countries or conjuring them on our mobile devices destabilises the local and intrinsic as the traditional purview of a culture traditionally embedded there. Even in migrant societies, a sense of the local had grown up over the generations which now, for some, seems threatened.

In the world as non-stop virtual reality show, in which my children are growing up, place is a fluid node of connectivity. Not yet 10, they have visited half of the ASEAN countries, several in Northeast Asia, the "Middle East", and Canada twice. Twenty-somethings navigate Singapore's streets hooked to something on their iPhones much as the young generation may have done 50 years ago with their ears plugged into a transistor radio. Late adolescent or early adult Singaporeans seem connected to some dream of universal "elsewhereness"; but the difference between the iPhone screen and the transistor radio of course is that the latter did not block out one's attention to one's surroundings, but merely gave it another soundtrack. The worldview of contemporary young adults is frequently cosmopolitan, with a near-obsession with mobility and the instant (quasi-, *Ersatz*) gratification of communications. Such a worldview may seem fractured, dissonant, the expression of an "age of distraction" as Jonathan Schell ably described it in a 1996 article.[2]

Right up to the mid-1960s, place was generally destiny. After the First World War, Thomas Hardy wrote an astonished poem "On One Who Lived and Died Where He was Born" — and he meant that quite specifically, in the same house. While Raffles, Farquhar and others of their century whose stories are told elsewhere have entered the iconography of Singapore, they were of course exceptions in their time. Common to most of his generation and at least his original class, my father (born in London's East End in 1912) left the UK only once in his life: to fight in the Second World War (he saw North Africa and Italy). My first flight, in 1968 [I was 13] was from London to Venice, and — a feat unfortunately scarcely to be repeated in later years — I and some of my friends got to sit in first class, which I remember today as more like a suburban train carriage, or those of the Hogwarts Express or Mr. Bean variety. Later that year, I was off on the *Queen Mary* to New York and the first of many sojourns in the US and Canada.

Yet for all the much trumped "death of distance" (the title of a 1997 Harvard Business School publication by Frances Cairncross), some constants remain, even though these too may initially appear to be changes. Immigrants are still held as suspect in some quarters, some superpower rivalries still obtain, and instability is still sown in certain sites across Southeast Asia. Classics Professor turned anti-immigration MP Enoch Powell still haunts the United Kingdom Independence party [UKIP], the main British anti-EU party, whose time had apparently come in 2014 and now is eclipsed. Climate change has become a mainstream interest, up

---

[2] Jonathan Schell, "Politics in an Age of Distraction," *Newsday*, 21 January 1996.

from a somewhat cranky obsession 50 years ago. Yet intergovernmental advocacy for climate adaptation and, if possible, mitigation is in some sense a morphing of trends set by Arne Naess, Rachel Carson and even John Muir in earlier generations. A concern with overpopulation has now reversed into a concern with a low birth rate. The absolute number of Singapore residents 0–9 years old is around the same as in 1980, although the total population has about doubled since then. There has been a marked increase in the population aged 20–40, but they do not seem to be getting married and having children at the same rate. Sociologists account for these well-known (and often lamented) figures in various ways, but the virtualised communities which might be taken to stand for the forging of more corporeal relationships may come back to haunt this generation in years ahead. Even if then the demographic trends (and similar could be noted for the EU) may appear very different, they can be brought back to one essential: in the estimation of policymakers and other like professionals (but not necessarily of a high percentage of the individuals who form the basis for the statistics and on whose behalf policy is formed), there is not enough population of the right age at the right time.

The rising generation is — as perhaps are all younger generations — confronted by a range of new threats. Among these are new clear and present dangers which radically and inexorably tear apart that virtual world to which we were becoming habituated, where everything and everyone, from friends to passers-by, were virtualised, "cloneable", along the lines of a real-world *Matrix* or *Oblivion*. While the youth of 1965 was growing up in a period of austerity, even aggression, the nature of these predicaments had been put in place some decades earlier, and therefore the relative novelty of the threats could be seen in some sense as traditional, or at least "known unknowns." Some of the early 21st-century threats can appear as transformations of old ones, e.g. the definition of terrorism in West Asia (in 1947 a *London News Chronicle* cartoon depicted Zionist terrorism as essentially self-defeating, the prey of a vulture), or the "new Cold War" after Russia's incursions into Ukraine. Yet while the longevity and provenance of the older forms of these conflicts diminished their unsettling characteristics (e.g. Russia — the USSR — was a threat because it had been Socialist — or in more popular and inexact parlance, "Communist" — since 1917), the new forms have not gelled into the social psyche so that their disconcerting aspects can be discounted.

In the summer of 1965, Betty Goetz Lall, who had been a senior administrative member of the US Senate Special Sub-Committee on Disarmament in the late 1950s, visited several countries in a wide arc from India to Japan, and including Malaysia and Singapore. The precise dates of her visit are not specified but her report, published in the *Bulletin of the Atomic Scientists* in November, lists the two places as separate countries. Preceding this visit, she had been in West Germany, the Federal Republic. So much has changed since then, of course: what was then divided (and this goes both for the current EU and ASEAN) is now united, at least solid frameworks for interdependence have been built. Big regional, even global players, like Germany and China, were not then members of the UN; for a while, Indonesia had "ceased cooperation" with what we now may consider a world body. Yet some of what Dr. Goetz Lall noted on her travels in certain Southeast Asian countries remains pertinent 50 years later: disputes in the area about territory; the importance in their resolution of negotiation over force; the significance of regional economic and political architecture to counterbalance hegemonic forces. On the German side, she noted a willingness of German youth to consider reunification (and this a mere four years after the Berlin Wall went up); this may have had to wait for another quarter century, but the desire was eventually accomplished, when a new generation of youth had taken their place. In late 2014, the ASEAN Economic Community was taking shape, and significant milestones should have been crossed by the end of 2015. And Germany remains very much committed to the European integration project. These developments may be grounds for cautious optimism for the next 50 years.

Dr. Barnard Turner is Senior Lecturer at the Department of English Language and Literature, Faculty of Arts and Social Sciences, National University of Singapore.

Debunking Some "Euromyths" — Understanding the European Union (EU) and Its Connections to Singapore

Loke Hoe Yeong

The European Union (EU) has often been the victim of myths bandied about in the popular consciousness. These have even earned the moniker of "Euromyths". Some of the most viral and hilarious ones may even be familiar to people in this part of the world:

"The EU will be banning the sale of eggs by the dozen."

"Curved bananas will be banned by the EU; only straight ones may be sold."

(Occasionally, the reverse myth that straight bananas would be banned in the EU has also been bandied about, which only reflects the state of confusion between myth and fact.)

The EU is a complex entity, given the very ambitious project of regional integration that has been ongoing in Europe since the end of World War II. Part of this involves the laborious standardisation of regulations across the continent when creating the Single Market. European Commission bureaucrats — christened "Eurocrats" — have sometimes been the unfortunate object of scorn by Eurosceptics across the EU. "The Eurocrats in Brussels are intruding on our daily lives yet again, telling us how to buy our bananas and eggs," so goes the cry of some European citizens.

In Singapore and Asia at large, misconceptions of the EU are common too. Of course, the preoccupation here has not been with bananas or eggs. Rather, the EU is generally perceived in this part of the world as being a less important political, security and economic actor than the US or China, or an actor that is almost absent from Asia. Academic studies on perceptions of the EU in Asia affirm that view. This is not surprising, some may say, since the EU is distant geographically. In the economic realm at least, the facts certainly do not support this assessment. So, in addressing some of the common perceptions (or misperceptions) of the EU, perhaps this article could help raise greater awareness of the EU and its connections to Singapore.

Below are just a sample of some Euromyths that one might come across from time to time when reading about the EU and following the discussions particularly in our mainstream media:

1. It is difficult to do business in Europe — the EU is too bureaucratic, and the markets are too tightly regulated.

There is perhaps no better way to respond to this than to invoke the EU's Single Market. In the words of the European Commission, the Single Market is about bringing down barriers to trade, and simplifying existing rules.

Trade is an exclusive competence of the European Commission, which acts on behalf of all EU member states. This actually makes trading with the 28 member states of the EU much more straightforward for external countries — there is just one set of trading rules and rule-makers for all 28 EU countries. A trade agreement with the EU means access to a single market of over 500 million consumers, and a single set of rules rather than 28 sets of rules.

Building the Single Market in Europe naturally involves the standardisation of regulations, harmonisation or mutual recognition of standards across the continent, and at times the long processes to achieve these. A contentious Business for Britain (BfB) report in 2013 stated that there have been 3,600 new EU laws in three years for businesses, and that it would take 92 days to read all the regulations. This statistic is debatable though. Moreover, there is no reason why a stuffed toy manufacturer needs to read up on fishing laws for instance, or indeed a vast majority of these regulations.

Whatever the state of red tape in the European Union is, it has not dissuaded external countries from trading with and investing in the EU. In 2013, the EU with a 15% share of global trade is the number one trading power (compare this to US's share — 12.9% and China's — 13.5%). The EU is also the biggest recipient of FDI and number one investor globally.

The EU has been one of the largest trading partners of Singapore in goods and services in recent times, surpassing the other economic giants, China and the US to be number one or number two trading partner. The EU was also ASEAN's second largest trading partner, after China, in 2013.

2. The EU does not think strategically; hence, it cannot be an effective security actor in Asia.

"Economic giant, political dwarf" — so goes the perception of some commentators about the EU. But the EU is more involved in Asia and ASEAN than most people think.

The EU has observer status at key regional forums in Asia, from the ASEAN Regional Forum to the South Asian Association for Regional Cooperation (SAARC). It has signed ASEAN's Treaty of Amity and Cooperation (TAC), a non-aggression pact. It has maintained a naval presence in the Indian Ocean known as Operation Atalanta, which deals with piracy off the coast of Somalia; in December 2014, this was extended for two more years. It once sent a monitoring mission to Aceh, to oversee the implementation of a peace agreement in the Indonesian province. It is the world's biggest aid donor, playing a major relief role in the 2004 Indian Ocean earthquake and tsunami disaster to floods in Pakistan. It has given €55.2 billion worth of overseas assistance in 2013.

Far from being an uninvolved actor in Asia, it could fairly be said that the EU has engaged Asia on different dimensions and at different levels, and is now trying to develop a comprehensive strategy towards Asia.

The charge of the EU's supposed absence from the Asian security arena largely stems from the comparison of its military presence in Asia to that of the US. But the EU has no rightful military role in Asia, unlike the US with its military alliances with Japan and South Korea that date back to the end of World War II. However, it can and has contributed to addressing several non-traditional security matters in Southeast Asia.

3. When it comes to international crises such as the conflict in Ukraine, and other international issues, policies, EU foreign policy is no different from US foreign policy — they are all "western countries" after all.

On the conflict in Ukraine, it is not true that EU foreign policy has all along been uniform with that of the US. It was not a straightforward task for the EU to cobble together a common stance to condemn Russia's annexation of Crimea and impose sanctions on Russia for its role in Eastern Ukraine. While the US was quick to impose sanctions, the EU needed to calibrate its response in view of the dependency of some EU countries on energy supplies from Russia, and diverse trade and commercial interests of EU member states. Some EU countries were also wary of enacting tough sanctions on Russian businesses, for fear of legal challenges in the European Court of Justice, after a series of such successful challenges from Iranian businesspersons. Nonetheless, a set of sanctions were agreed upon, and the EU has stuck to these sanctions while exploring ways to continue dialogue with Russia to find a political solution to the crisis in Ukraine.

On other issues such as the International Criminal Court and climate change, the differences between the EU's and the US's policies are well known. On the latter, the EU has been adamant in meeting its obligations under the Kyoto Protocol, applying mandatory laws and regulations, whereas the US did not even ratify the Protocol and was resistant towards negotiating a legally binding international climate change treaty post-Kyoto. The US also did not support the creation of the International Criminal Court.

4. Politics in Europe is poisoned by the rise of far-right parties in European Parliament elections.

Even casual observers are aware of the news of far-right parties gaining ground in the recent European Parliament elections of May 2014. The history of fascism in Europe on the eve of World War II has perhaps coloured the general perception of Europe's susceptibility to far-right movements. But Europe is not alone here — there has been a rise of nationalism and right-wing politics in Asia in recent years too. One just has to witness how some Asian countries and governments have reacted vis-à-vis the maritime disputes in the East and South China Seas.

The performance of far-right parties in European and national elections has tended to fluctuate over the years. There has not been any consistent trend in their growth. The periods of their rise are generally correlated to socioeconomic factors such as high unemployment rates, and indeed Europe is emerging from such an economic crisis.

Even though a far-right party like Marine Le Pen's Front National of France has increased its share of seats in the European Parliament to 24 to become the largest French party represented, others like Geert Wilders' Party for Freedom (PVV in Dutch) of the Netherlands have conversely seen their support stagnate at four seats at the same elections. These two parties had even forged an alliance for the recent European elections, yet their fortunes could not have been more different. Rather than a straightforward surge in far-right sentiments among the European electorate, this seems to indicate that more nuanced explanations are needed. The electoral results really did boil down to the specific circumstances of each party in each EU member state.

Another explanation touches on one of the weaknesses of the European Parliament's standing, admittedly — European voters still somehow regard European elections as a "second-order contest" (to use Karlheinz Reif and Hermann Schmitt's much-cited term from their 1980 article) compared to their own national elections. The rationale here is that because national leaders still matter more in terms of political decisions affecting the lives of European citizens, voters are more inclined to vote astutely in national elections, while they regard European elections as a means to exercise a protest vote. Turnout for European Parliament elections has tended to be lower than that for national elections too. This could be read as a tactical way for the European voter to exert political pressure on their national leaders, while retaining support for mainstream, tried-and-tested parties in their own national governments.

Nonetheless, the EU has been giving the European Parliament more powers and responsibilities over the years, so that their work really matters. One of these is increased oversight powers for the European Parliament over international treaties signed by the EU, such as free trade agreements.

5. The United Kingdom emerged more strongly out of the financial crisis than other EU countries because it has opted out of many EU initiatives — the single currency, the Schengen area — thus giving it sovereign control to fix and safeguard its economy.

The reality is of course not that simplistic. UK was of course in better control of its monetary and fiscal policies and able to devalue the pound. But at the same time it also embarked on a course of austerity as with many other EU member states, and has emerged more strongly from the crisis.

Indeed with the single currency, Eurozone countries are no longer able to independently devalue their currencies in order to restore competitiveness. But as some economists have pointed out, it is precisely this feature of the single currency that has averted a deeper crisis of "competitive" devaluation in Europe. If crisis-stricken countries in Europe had drastically devalued their currencies in a state of confused panic, it could have led to hyperinflation across the continent, and the consequences for the global economy might have been worse.

It should also be recalled that British banks were some of the first in Europe to be hit by the crisis, because of their greater exposure to the US capital markets, where the crisis originated with the collapse of Lehmann Brothers. Arguably, the UK emerged relatively unscathed from the crisis, not because it was "unhampered" by the euro or other EU initiatives, but in then Prime Minister Gordon Brown's key decision to bail out the ailing bank Northern Rock in 2008, as well as adopting several austerity measures.

The debates about the UK's continued membership in the EU have prompted the current British government to promise an in/out referendum on EU membership for 2017. The business community has been consistently clear on what it wants though — for instance, a widely publicised 2013 report by TheCityUK showed unambiguously that 84% of business leaders in the UK want their country to stay in the EU.

In conclusion, one could ask why there is this preponderance of myths about the EU in the popular consciousness. Fingers have often been pointed at the so-called "Anglo-Saxon press". More specifically, it is the Eurosceptic British tabloids that have been blamed for the proliferation of Euromyths. The intention of mythbusting here is not to be an apologist for the EU. But given the importance of the EU as a key trading partner and investor in Singapore, and the increasing desire of the EU to strengthen its presence in Southeast Asia, it is certainly worth getting the record straight on some of these common misperceptions.

Loke Hoe Yeong is an Associate Fellow of the EU Centre.

The Asia-Europe Meeting (ASEM): A Bridge between East and West

Goh Chok Tong

When I became Prime Minister of Singapore in 1990, the Cold War had ended and the world was transiting to a new order. Asia was experiencing a period of unprecedented high economic growth: Japan and the so-called "Asian Tigers" — Hong Kong, Singapore, South Korea and Taiwan — led this wave, followed by the re-emergence of China and India. In Europe, the entry into force of the Maastricht Treaty on 1 November 1993 laid a firm foundation for closer economic and financial integration. With the collapse of the Soviet Union and the ascendency of North America, East Asia and Western Europe, a tri-polar world order was taking shape.

I was of the view that if we could connect these three economic blocs together like a triangle, the result would be a more stable geopolitical environment for all. North America and Europe already had longstanding institutional linkages, by virtue of their shared history and culture. North America and East Asia had also begun to forge closer ties under the aegis of the Asia-Pacific Economic Cooperation (APEC). However, the missing institutional link that was needed to complete the triangle was closer relations between Asia and Europe.

Europe's interest in Asia had dwindled after the withdrawals of France from Indochina and of the UK from territories east of the Suez in the last century. On Asia's part, colonisation had dampened its enthusiasm for closer relations with Europe. Partly because of this, Western Europe was trading and investing less in Asia than in the US. In 1994, North America accounted for 25% of the EU's total trade volume, whereas its total trade with 10 countries in East Asia (Brunei, Indonesia, Malaysia, the Philippines, Singapore, Thailand, Vietnam, China, Japan and South Korea) made up only 8% of the total.

The World Economic Forum (WEF) Europe/East Asia Summit held in Singapore in October 1994 provided an occasion for me to seed the idea of closer dialogue between Asia and Europe at the leaders' level. European leaders then had limited contacts with a China which was not yet fully opened to foreign investments and imports. In its July 1994 Communique, "Towards a New Asia Strategy", the European Commission sought to "accord Asia a higher priority than is at present the case" and to "strengthen its economic presence in Asia in order to maintain its leading role in the world economy". Similarly, Asia wanted Europe's investments and access to its markets. Given Singapore's close relations with ASEAN, China and the rest of the Asia-Pacific as well as with Europe, I thought that we were well placed to seed the idea of an Asia-Europe Meeting (ASEM).

During my official visit to France in October 1994, I proposed to Prime Minister Édouard Balladur the idea of establishing a regular summit for leaders from Europe and Asia to meet, to get to know each other and to develop ties between the two regions. He was receptive. The French were due to assume the EU Presidency in January 1995. Prime Minister Balladur undertook to sell the idea to the EU member states, and I, in turn, did likewise with Asian leaders. I secured the ASEAN leaders' support for ASEM a month later on the sidelines of the APEC summit in Bogor, Indonesia. Later, we secured China, Japan and South Korea's buy-in. On their part, the French delivered their side of the bargain. The inaugural ASEM summit was launched with great success in Bangkok in March 1996. 15 countries from Europe and 10 countries from Asia participated. The European Commission was also present. Our discussions were candid, fresh, free-flowing and productive. The informal nature of the dialogue allowed leaders to establish a high level of comfort and familiarity with one another. It proved to be one of ASEM's abiding strengths.

ASEM — Vision and Reality

This proved fortuitous as ASEM was tested very early after its birth, when Asia was hit badly by the Asian Financial Crisis in 1997. At the second ASEM summit in London in 1998, Europe sought to understand the genesis of the Asian Financial Crisis and showed concern and continued interest in its Asian partners. Our European partners demonstrated their commitment to Asia and the ASEM process by establishing the ASEM Trust Fund at this summit. It was a show of faith.

As the EU took on new members, ASEM's membership inevitably expanded. The cosiness of the early summits was lost. ASEM came under severe criticism for the lack of focus and substance. Interventions became increasingly scripted and mundane, and several ASEM summits showed poor attendance. But I think this diffusion of ASEM's focus was only one part of the story. A more important reason was the increased direct contact between European and Chinese leaders after China lifted its bamboo curtain. ASEM as a meeting venue for them had lost its salience. Another reason was the preoccupation of European leaders with more pressing domestic and EU problems. ASEM cohesion was also tested when Myanmar's application to join ASEM was blocked by the European partners. Both sides locked horns on this for a while. It was finally resolved with the admission of Myanmar in 2004.

We should not lose faith in the founding vision and value of ASEM. As the meeting point of a resurgent Asia and institutionally important Europe, Asian and European leaders continue to see ASEM's long-term strategic value. I am therefore confident that ASEM will continue to remain relevant.

Since its founding, ASEM's operating environment has been fundamentally altered by the Asian renaissance, the Eurozone crisis and recently, the global war on terror. Whatever else may change, ASEM's raison d'être of strengthening Asia-Europe links remains. Trade agreements such as the Trans-Pacific Partnership (TPP) and the Transatlantic Trade and Investment Partnership (TTIP), once in force, will propel the economic ties between Asia and the US, and Europe and the US respectively. But there is no similar initiative between Asia and Europe yet. ASEM therefore holds the key to realising an Asia-Europe answer to the TPP and TTIP.

ASEM should also tap on the diverse civilisational strengths of Asia and Europe to address global challenges, such as climate change, nuclear non-proliferation, and the rise of radical Islam, which uses terror, violence and killings to advance its cause. The diversity of input can only add to a more nuanced understanding of the issues and the perspectives of different countries. This in turn will enhance the resilience of individual ASEM partners to these challenges.

These are major undertakings that will occupy not only the current generation of leaders, but also future generations. Yet, leaders are not permanent members of ASEM; only their countries are. All the more cause then, for a forum like ASEM, for old, new and future leaders to continually develop their ties and understanding of each region's challenges and aspirations.

Our interactions over the last two decades have laid a strong tradition for this process to continue. ASEM has thrived as a dialogue forum because of its informality and flexibility. I think that we should not seek to transform ASEM into a more structured and bureaucratic body. Given its large size and diverse membership, ASEM's objectives are best served by fostering collegial dialogue and a genuine desire for cooperation. ASEM should continue to be viewed as a process.

The Next Lap

Singapore is deeply committed to the ASEM process and will contribute its energy and ideas to ensure that ASEM remains credible and effective. Singapore will also continue to support the Asia-Europe Foundation in its mission to strengthen people-to-people ties, and cultural and academic exchanges between the two regions.

As ASEM sets to commemorate its 20th anniversary in 2016, its future looks bright. ASEM continues to attract new members — Croatia and Kazakhstan were admitted into ASEM in 2014, bringing ASEM's total membership to 53. Turkey and Ukraine have also started their applications. These facts are a testament to ASEM's continued value. Indeed, ASEM has effectively become a commonwealth of nations from Europe and Asia!

As a community of Asian and European nations, I believe that there is much untapped potential in ASEM. We should continue to strengthen our side of the triangle. In the words of Rudyard Kipling, *"there is neither East nor West, Border, nor Breed, nor Birth, When two strong men stand face to face, tho' they come from the ends of the earth"*. Europe and Asia must celebrate differences even as they explore common grounds. As the EU and Asia continue to deepen their respective regional integration, they should also look beyond their immediate region and create synergistic opportunities. Such habits of cooperation have only positives and no negatives. They will reinforce the peace and prosperity that our people need to lead a rich, balanced and fulfilling life.

Goh Chok Tong is Emeritus Senior Minister, Singapore. He was Prime Minister of Singapore from 1990–2004.

Singapore and the Asia-Europe Foundation (ASEF)

Tommy Koh and Peggy Kek

In memory of Edmond Israel, Horst Krenzler and Jay-Hee Oh[1]

Introduction

The establishment of the Asia-Europe Foundation (ASEF) was one of Singapore's most significant and concrete contributions to people-to-people relations between Asia and Europe.

At a meeting of senior officials in Dublin in December 1996, ASEM (Asia-Europe Meeting) members adopted by consensus the so-called Dublin Principles that would form the foundation of ASEF. Singapore offered to host the Foundation and a year after the first Asia-Europe Meeting took place in Bangkok, ASEF was launched in Singapore in February 1997, by the 26 founding members of ASEM.

ASEF's first home was a gracious black and white bungalow with extensive grounds at No. 1 Nassim Hill, within walking distance of the Singapore Botanic Gardens. As we were the founding Executive Director and Director of Public Affairs respectively, we had the great pleasure of working in that beautiful office from 1997 to 2000.

Unique Mandate

We found those three years exhilarating. There was much to be done, and much that could be done. As far as we could tell, there was no other organisation in the world like ASEF.

While there are other organisations that aim to promote understanding between countries, they mostly do so on behalf of only one country, albeit reaching out to many others. Examples of these are the Alliance Française, British Council, Goethe

---

[1] Edmond Israel, Horst Krenzler and Jay-Hee Oh were, respectively, the first ASEF Governors for Luxembourg, the European Commission and South Korea.

Institute, Confucius Institute, Instituto Cervantes, Istituto Italiano di Cultura and Nehru Centre.

Although the Commonwealth institutions seek in some way to promote understanding among multiple countries, the member countries all share a common history of having been part of the British Empire and speaking the same language.

On the other hand, ASEM membership was based on a shared vision, born in Bangkok, to reconnect two important regions and civilisations of the world. Initially, the membership was confined to the European Union, ASEAN and three states of Northeast Asia, namely, China, Japan and South Korea.

Sense of Ownership

As members of the start-up team, we had the challenge and the opportunity to introduce ASEF to the world. We had to convince institutions in ASEM member countries to work with us. To them, ASEF was an unknown quantity. To succeed, we knew that we would need the support of enthusiastic and loyal champions. We were fortunate that we had some early believers, who, in turn, helped us to win over more supporters.

We needed to raise the profile of ASEF quickly, encourage participation in our projects and events, and give ASEM members a sense of ownership of ASEF.

This last need was particularly difficult to fulfil as ASEF had a physical presence only in Singapore, on Nassim Hill. We avoided the easy option of holding all the projects in Singapore and instead worked extra hard to find relevant and willing partners in as many different countries and to involve participants from as many member countries as possible.

We were greatly helped by a supportive board. The first two ASEF governors for Singapore were Dr. Yeo Ning Hong and Mr. J. Y. Pillay, who trusted and provided useful advice to the management team. Prof. Helmut Haussmann, who has been the ASEF Governor for Germany since 1997, was instrumental in opening doors to German parliamentarians, think tanks and foundations. The late Mr. Edmond Israel ensured that we had a direct line to the political leadership of Luxembourg. The late Ambassador Jay-Hee Oh played a critical role in the success of ASEF's work at ASEM II, in Seoul, in October 2000.

We partnered organisations that had more established reputations and networks. In these respects, it greatly helped that Singapore was both an important destination for the world's political and business leaders and that Singaporean institutions were part of many international networks. When the Asian Financial Crisis occurred in 1998, it was felt in many of the affected Asian countries that the crisis had been misunderstood by some Western countries and institutions including the IMF. So, taking advantage of the pulling power of the World Economic Forum (WEF) and the presence of Europe's media in Singapore for the WEF East Asia Summit, ASEF initiated a Colloquium for Journalists for a discussion on how Europe could help Asia without creating a backlash.

With the help of the National University of Singapore and INSEAD, we were able to organise, at the latter's Fontainebleau campus in France, a conference to discuss the idea of an Asia-Europe Education Hub. With that, a new network of Asian and European universities was launched.

Building Bridges and Networks

We set about our mission by being a creator of new networks, an interpreter of key developments and events, and an intellectual bridge-builder. Our strategy included making sure that the projects we organised were relevant and newsworthy. In all these efforts, Singapore institutions and individuals from think tanks, the arts and cultural sector, and the media were amongst our earliest supporters. Amongst these were the late Kuo Pao Kun, Haresh Sharma, Ong Keng Sen, Kenson Kwok, Lee Tsao Yuan, Arun Mahizhnan, Asad Latif and, Goh Ching Lee. We also worked closely with colleagues from the National Heritage Board, MediaCorp, Straits Times and many other institutions.

We created new Asia-Europe networks of arts groups, museums, parliamentarians, school students, universities, teachers, journalists and researchers. Many of these networks have continued to thrive with the support of subsequent ASEF management teams.

We also initiated projects that helped to explain significant developments in both regions such as the Asian financial crisis in 1998 and the advent of the Euro. When Indonesia was preparing for its first democratic elections in 1999, ASEF created a platform to help Europe better understand the historic event taking place in the most populous nation in Southeast Asia. We assembled a panel comprising representatives from all the major parties and invited journalists from all the ASEM countries to Jakarta to attend the Colloquium.

As an intellectual bridge-builder, we convened discussions on issues that often divided politicians and intellectuals of Asia and Europe, issues such as human rights and the question of Myanmar (also known as Burma). We also organised a seminar in Paris, with the support of the French Ministry of Finance, to discuss the causes of the Asian financial crisis and the prospects of Asia, post-crisis.

Early Challenges and Champions

Besides Singapore, France and Luxembourg were also among the early champions of ASEF. Like Singapore, the two countries made substantial financial contributions to help ASEF get off to a good start. In addition, France also provided Pierre Barroux as the deputy executive director of ASEF.

In 1999, when Europeans were getting ready to launch the euro, ASEF initiated a roadshow to provide Europe with a platform to introduce the Euro to Asia. We took the roadshow to Hong Kong, Beijing and Singapore with Jean-Claude Trichet, Christian Noyer and Dominique Strauss-Kahn. Mr. Trichet was the President of the European Central Bank, Mr. Noyer was the President of the central bank of France and Mr. Strauss-Kahn was the Finance Minister of France. This project could not have succeeded without the strong support of the government of France.

Luxembourg hosted the first Asia-Europe Editors' Meeting in October 1997. The meeting was a wonderful platform to present ASEF to some 30 members of the media of Asia and Europe. Some of the editors we met at that first meeting became some of ASEF's most ardent supporters. Among them were Mr. Felix Soh of Singapore's *Straits Times*, Mr. Larry Jagan, the founding editor of BBC World Service's East Asia Today programme, Ms. Shada Islam, formerly with the *Far Eastern Economic Review*, Mr. Matthias Nass, the Editor of *Die Zeit* (Germany), Kavi Chongkittavorn of *The Nation* (Thailand), and Ambassador Sabam Siagian, the publisher of the *Jakarta Post* (Indonesia). They remain great friends and supporters of ASEF and we were happy to learn that subsequent teams of ASEF have continued to maintain relations with this informal network and to organise annual editions of the Asia-Europe Editors' Meeting.

Enduring ASEF Flagship Projects

Despite the changes in membership and management teams, some projects that were launched in the initial years of ASEF have not only survived the years, but are in fact flourishing.

The ASEF Editors Roundtable is now a mainstay event organised biennially on the sidelines of every ASEM Summit. The ASEF Journalists' Colloquium continues to bring the media together for significant developments and now has a regular scheduled spot on the sidelines of the ASEM Foreign Ministers' Meeting.

The ASEF Classroom Network (ASEF ClassNet) continues to foster collaboration among secondary and high school teachers and students in Asia and Europe. The ASEM Education Hub is now known as the ASEF Higher Education Programme, and has given birth to four sub-programmes:

- ASEM Rectors' Conference (ARC) and Students' Forum
- Asia-Europe Education Workshops
- ASEM Education and Research Hub for Lifelong Learning (ASEM LLL Hub)
- Database on Education Exchange Programmes (DEEP)

The ASEM Museum Network continues to thrive. The ASEM Informal Seminar on Human Rights continues to bring government officials, academics and civil society representatives from Asia and Europe for dialogues on difficult issues.

Major Changes Since 2000

ASEF has undergone many changes since 2000, when we stepped down. With these changes, there have been new opportunities and challenges.

One of the biggest changes is the number of ASEM members. From 26 members in 1997, ASEM now has 53 members. This development alone has had significant implications on the way ASEF operates. As the founding principles had a provision for every ASEM member to be represented on the ASEF board of governors, this has made ASEF board meetings a much bigger undertaking now, both logistically and in agenda-setting.

On the positive side, this expansion means that there are, potentially, many more sources of support, both intellectual and financial. It also means that there are more countries to reach out to, more countries in which to raise the profile of ASEF, and more countries among which to spread the projects. This also makes it much harder for ASEF to gain traction in each specific country.

Despite all the challenges it faces, ASEF continues to grow from strength to strength. The current management team has identified new areas of focus that are relevant to today's world. Two of the new themes to have emerged are public health and sustainable development.

Conclusion

Over the years, many Singaporeans have served and continue to serve on the board of governors, management team and staff of ASEF. Today, 18 years after its establishment, ASEF remains the only brick and mortar institution of ASEM. It has played a unique and significant role in enhancing mutual understanding between Asia and Europe.

If ASEM members believe in the mission of ASEF, we sincerely hope that they will demonstrate this by making substantial and regular financial contributions to sustain the Foundation. After all, every ASEM member has a representative on the ASEF board and has a say in the direction and work plan of ASEF. Every ASEM member therefore has the responsibility to help ASEF thrive and succeed.

On Singapore's part, we have no doubt that its government and people will continue to uphold and provide staunch support for the mission of ASEF, and for the aspirations of ASEM to build strong and meaningful multilateral relations with Europe.

Professor Tommy Koh and Ms. Peggy Kek were respectively the Executive Director and Director of Public Affairs of ASEF from 1997 to 2000.

Singapore, Germany and the European Union — Political Dialogue for Closer Cooperation and Mutual Understanding

Wilhelm Hofmeister

Germans like Singapore. They appreciate the cleanliness, the greenery, the security and the smooth functioning of many public services, which begins the moment you arrive into the country, with the efficient passport control and baggage handling at Changi airport. Germans also like the dynamics and constant strive for innovation and improvement in Singapore, making it a benchmark for the entire Southeast Asian region.

This mutual respect and the appreciation for cooperation between both countries are manifested in various fields. A simple example: Singaporean jazz pianist and Cultural Medallion recipient Jeremy Monteiro invited two German musicians with whom he had performed many times before in Singapore, Germany and other parts of the world to his Christmas concert 2014 in the Esplanade Concert hall. Comparably, the Singapore Symphony Orchestra and other local artists have also often performed in Germany. This is just one indicator of the many bonds and friendships shared between our countries. Those personal relations are built by many of the 7,000 Germans who live in the garden city-state, including the representatives of 1,400 German companies and over 200 scientists.

Cooperation in the field of science and education is one of the pillars of the relationship between our two countries. More than 50 bilateral cooperation agreements between German and Singapore universities support scientific collaboration. In 2002, the Technical University of Munich established its first "independent foreign subsidiary" — the "German Institute of Science and Technology (GIST-TUM Asia)" in Singapore. It now offers undergraduate and postgraduate degrees as well as doctoral and research programmes in cooperation with

Singaporean universities and polytechnics. Additionally, many young people from Singapore go to German universities and vice versa every year. This brings our countries closer together — although Singaporeans might suffer a bit more because they have to learn the German language and cope with the colder weather in our country. But the prospect of studying at a good university abroad with subsequent good career possibilities is certainly worth the effort.

Business and politics provide another dimension for bilateral relations. Singapore is Germany's most important economic partner in Southeast Asia. Both countries focus on an open world economy, free trade and reliable investment conditions, which is crucial in promoting growth and employment. According to Singapore's statistics, exports to Germany amounted to 4.43 billion euros in 2013, while imports from Germany reached 8.24 billion euros. This means that Germany was once again Singapore's most important trading partner within the EU in 2013. Investments from Germany were as high as 8 billion euros. Institutions such as the Singaporean-German Chamber of Commerce (SGC), German Centre Singapore and German-Singaporean Business Forum (GSBF) in Singapore, and the offices of the Economic Development Board (EDB) as well as International Enterprise Singapore (IE Singapore) in Frankfurt am Main contribute to the economic activities and have helped shape the relations for more than two decades. Together, Germany and Singapore are engaged in an open and reliable framework at the global level.

In the political arena, bilateral relations are characterised by trust and mutual understanding. German Chancellors Helmut Schmidt (1974–1982), Helmut Kohl (1982–1998), Gerhard Schröder (1998–2007) and Angela Merkel (since 2005) have maintained close personal relations with the Prime Ministers of Singapore, sometimes even to the extent of personal friendship as in the case of Helmut Schmidt and Lee Kuan Yew. Prime Minister Lee Hsien Loong's visit to Germany in February 2014 confirmed the continuous good personal relations between the leaders of both countries.

Moreover, our countries' relations are based on close cooperation in multilateral affairs. Germany values Singapore's constructive position within ASEAN and its role as a facilitator and promoter of political relations between European and Asian countries. It was former Prime Minister Goh Chok Tong of Singapore who initiated the Asia-Europe Meeting (ASEM) — today's main forum for multilateral engagement between the regions.

Germany and Singapore also agree on major foreign policy issues such as the need for global and regional alliances for peacekeeping and to support the fight against terrorism. On the German side, there is an expectation that the Free Trade Agreement between the European Union and Singapore, and the upcoming partnership agreement, will only make the mutual relations even more dynamic.

Regional Integration

Regional integration is another issue which concerns both, although the context may differ. Both countries are economic powerhouses in their respective regions. But both Singapore and Germany also understand that in the context of international competition and uncertainties, countries can only maintain the current high levels of development and strength through close cooperation with regional neighbours. Therefore, we share the need to promote economic development and prosperity in our respective neighbourhoods through regional integration and cooperation which are beneficial for our own economies while enhancing regional security concurrently.

In Europe, the debris and traumatic experiences of World War II fostered the desire for regional integration. In 1945, politicians such as former French Foreign Minister Robert Schuman, Italy's Prime Minister Alcide De Gasperi and German Chancellor Konrad Adenauer began building new trust between European countries by experimenting with new forms of cooperation and integration. In a very early stage of integration, new institutions were created to organise and even guide the integration process. Over the decades, Europeans have established additional institutions, delegated more and more powers to them and weakened national competencies for the overall enlargement of the Union with now 28 Member States. This enhancement of supranational institutions was thought to be necessary in order to enable common governance in many areas.

In Southeast Asia, five countries came together in 1967, also to build trust and ward off the threat of communism and political interference. Singapore is a founding member of the Association of Southeast Asian Nations (ASEAN) with the aim to strengthen security and stability in the region. In the framework of ASEAN, some institutions have been created such as the ASEAN Secretariat, and ASEAN has also grown from five to ten members. Into the 21st century, ASEAN is also moving towards deepening its regional cooperation. More regional institutions have been created but ASEAN members have, unlike the EU, resisted the idea of transferring competences to regional institutions. ASEAN remains very much an intergovernmental organisation.

For both Germany and Singapore, the development of the EU and ASEAN, and progress in regional integration for peace and prosperity are prominent topics in their national agendas. To facilitate mutual policy learning in regional integration, political dialogue is crucial and provides the perfect platform for further mutual cooperation between both countries and regions.

Political Dialogue Singapore-Europe

Political dialogue is an appropriate instrument both for comparative analysis and for the exchange of experiences as well as ideas on commonalities shared between

Singapore, Germany and Europe. Such dialogue can also help address many of today's complex challenges, which cannot be managed by one country alone — such as the issue of climate change — with its aims to promote and enhance governance and international understanding, or the issue of migration which signifies a serious challenge for the European Union in these days.

Climate Change and Energy

Climate change and its consequences are one of the biggest challenges for international politics and cooperation. Although there is no doubt about the devastating effects of climate change for many countries, international negotiations are characterised by strategies which are still primarily driven by national interests. Examples of this can be found in Europe and Asia alike. Nevertheless, it was the Singaporean and German Ministers for Environment — Vivian Balakrishnan and Peter Altmaier — who fostered the negotiation results of COP18 in Doha which underlined both countries' international commitment. With its advanced technological development, Singapore can play an even bigger role in Asia by exemplifying the view that economic development does not have to be accompanied by increasing emissions of greenhouse gases — a typical dilemma for many emerging markets and developing countries that requires a clear decoupling strategy.

Closely linked to climate change is urbanisation. Cities are among the biggest polluters, while being particularly vulnerable to the effects of climate change. They can also provide the solutions to mitigate climate change. Thus, sustainable urbanisation is in the interest of both regions. Singapore has implemented a number of innovative policies and new technologies to improve urban living. Europe and Germany have vast experience in redesigning existing cities in a more eco-friendly manner. Through political dialogue the countries not only share their experiences, but may also provide new business opportunities for their companies abroad.

Another crucial issue area to address in climate discussions is energy. In order to avoid the mistakes of other countries, political dialogue can provide assistance. Asia will need to meet the demand generated by increased energy consumption through enhanced energy efficiency and an evolved energy mix. This has to see a higher share of renewable energies and a decentralised, small-scale energy production model. Focusing on environmental protection should not lead the countries to accept the next best alternative which might have even more destructive long-term effects. The current discussion on the promotion of nuclear energy in Asia is certainly not the only solution to the growing energy demand. The solution instead requires a comprehensive policy framework to support renewable energies, such as putting in place policies to support research and development and perhaps making the use of renewable energy compulsory in some areas.

Migration and Integration

Another commonality is the fact that our two countries have a relatively high proportion of migrants. In Singapore, almost 40% of the total population are transient migrant labour or permanent residents. But even among the 60% of citizens is a relatively high number of naturalised foreign-born people. In Germany, the total percentage of foreigners is approximately 8%, but another 12% of the population have a so-called migrant background, i.e. these are nationalised migrants with a German passport or their descendants have a German passport. In addition Germany receives many refugees from various regions of the world, seeking political asylum. Although they are not considered migrants, they remain temporarily or permanently in the country. In 2014 alone, nearly 200,000 people arrived and applied for asylum in Germany. Therefore, dealing with the migration phenomenon presents a challenge for our societies.

Additionally, both countries face the challenge of low fertility and an ageing society, which is why migrants are needed to maintain our levels of economic and social development. This requires an open as well as welcoming culture towards migrants. In both countries, this process is accompanied by critical comments and discussions. In Germany, legislative reforms and numerous public, private and social initiatives aim to give rise to a "welcoming culture" that facilitates the integration of foreigners. By now, most Germans accept that the economic rise and economic strength are also due to the contribution of immigrants. Nevertheless, there are also critical voices and political groups who wish to tighten the control on migration, denying the benefit of migration because of "increasing" competition. Such movements have raised questions about whether the government, political parties, business sector and all other organisations involved in the integration of foreigners may have failed to explain why we need migrants and what are the benefits of a multicultural society.

In an open society, as in Germany, there must be an open public debate on this issue, showing the advantages of migration while addressing the criticisms and challenges associated with migration in order to reach a compromise for all. In Singapore, immigration has also played a key role in building its economic strength. The majority of the population is aware of the important contributions made by migrants and welcomes their presence. This does not mean that criticism of this open door policy is absent. During the 2011 general elections, a widespread expression of discontent with the then immigration policies could be observed. Some seem to fear the competition with foreign-born residents at the labour and property markets and were dismayed with the pressure on public infrastructure and services as a result of the fast-paced immigration. Despite some policy tweaks by the Singapore government, criticism remains.

As a foreign observer, one can see a dilemma that is not so easy to overcome: on the one hand, the government knows that the country still needs a continuous influx of migrants to further develop its economic potential; on the other hand, it has tightened the conditions for immigration in order to meet the concerns of parts of its population. It turns out that we are struggling with similar challenges. Even if the specific circumstances differ, it is certainly worthwhile to hold political dialogues on these issues to learn from each other and possibly improve decisions on migration policies on both sides.

The Role of the Konrad-Adenauer-Stiftung

The Konrad-Adenauer-Stiftung (Foundation) is one of the institutions that promote and facilitate opportunities and platforms for political dialogue. We are pleased and grateful that we can work in Singapore and organise international meetings and dialogues from here, both in Singapore and in other Asian countries, involving representatives of various European and Asian countries.

As a German organisation, we obviously work based on our own values and norms. We represent the ideals of an open and democratic society. We are aware that societies are usually characterised by a variety of conflicts and diverse interests. We are nonetheless convinced that such conflicts can be best managed through open discussions aimed at a compromise, which tries to meet the diverse interests. This also applies to international cooperation. In Singapore, however, the idea of harmony is emphasised very strongly over conflict. Open conflict and noisy controversies about public policies are sometimes frowned upon. Nevertheless, in international relations as well as in national politics controversies are a natural element in the search for best policies. Political dialogue and debates can contribute to better policies. Political dialogue requires people to listen, to be open towards other perspectives and hear from people as well as countries of different size and status. In this way political dialogue will be mutually beneficial for all.

Therefore, with its 50th anniversary, one wishes Singapore not only well and more success in its impressive development, but political fortitude in coping with the impending sociopolitical challenges ahead.

Happy Birthday Singapore!

Dr. Wilhelm Hofmeister is Director of Political Dialogue Program Asia and Regional Representative, Konrad Adenauer Stiftung.

Section 2

Enduring Bilateral Ties

Belgians in Singapore: Helping to Write the City-State's (Hi)story

Gerard Cockx

The festivities marking Singapore's 50th anniversary kicked off on 4 January with a percussion concert in the Botanic Gardens. It featured Chinese, Malay, Indian and Eurasian percussion instruments. Belgian-born, and now proud Singapore citizen, Robert Casteels directed this rousing celebration of Singapore's multicultural and multi-ethnic identity.

On 9 August, the festivities will culminate in the National Day Parade, to be held on the Padang. Judging by last year's parade, we will be in for a very spectacular event. There is of course a lot to celebrate. Thanks to the vision of its leaders and the resourcefulness of its citizens, the city-state has been able to build on its strengths and turn its weaknesses into opportunities. In only a few decades, Singapore has gone from being a third-world country to one of the most developed first-world ones. As Sudhir Thomas Vadaketh writes in *Floating on a Malayan Breeze*, "Singapore is *the* economic success story of the past 50 years, bar none."[1] Over the years, Belgian citizens and companies have witnessed these developments and in many instances have been privileged to contribute to them.

As diplomats we rarely engage in alternate history ("what if ..."). But, what if the King of Spain in the early 17th century had decided to build a city on the *Isla de la Sabandaría Vieja* (the Island of the Old Portmaster's House) as Singapore was known then in the kingdom. This advice was given to him by Jacobus van de Koutere (aka Jacques de Coutre), an independent gem trader from Bruges in what is now Belgium. Van de Koutere, escaping the difficult religious and political atmosphere in his home country, spent nearly three decades travelling and trading in Asia. According to Peter Borschberg, the editor of *The Memoirs and Memorials*

---

[1] Sudhir Thomas Vadaketh, *Floating on a Malayan Breeze: Travels in Malaysia and Singapore* (Hong Kong: HKU Press, 2012), 145.

of Jacques de Coutre, he was to give the single most comprehensive European account of Singapore before 1800, well before Stamford Raffles set foot in Singapore.[2]

Against the background of the rivalry in Southeast Asia between the Spanish and the Portuguese on the one hand, and the Dutch on the other, van de Koutere counselled his Spanish master to not only build a city and acquire sovereignty over '*Lange Eyland* (or: the Long Island; Pulau Panjang), but also construct two fortresses, one on the main island (between Bedok and Changi Point), the other on the *Isla de Arena* (Sand Island or Sentosa). The latter "would be very useful and could serve as a safe refuge for ships from China".[3]

Away from his geostrategic musings, Jacobus was also a keen observer of the region's flora and fauna. In one instance he describes "local fruits which are very different from the fruits in Europe"; he is of course referring to the *duriones* (yes, durians). According to our man, they were "very healthy and very tasty"![4]

In the end, reportedly due to the overwhelming presence of the Dutch in Asian waters, these plans were abandoned. And Europeans forgot that durians were ever considered tasty (finding solace, instead, in blue cheese).

Fast forward to today's Singapore. Ever since the days of Jacobus van de Koutere and Stamford Raffles, its strategic location has always remained its main strength. But the weaknesses, as described by Lee Kuan Yew in his memoirs, were striking: lack of a hinterland, and no natural resources, except for its people. However, these people had determination and vision, and a willingness to learn from others. Chan Chin Bock writes in *Heart Work* how Goh Keng Swee, Singapore's "economic architect", requested the UN to send a team of experts from smaller developed nations to advise Singapore on its economic development.[5] Belgium, together with the Netherlands, Sweden and Israel, put experts on this team, which would lay the groundwork for Singapore's remarkable take-off.

As former Belgian Ambassador to Singapore Patrick Van Haute writes in the latest instalment of *The Little Red Dot: Reflections of Foreign Ambassadors on Singapore*, Singapore's success over the past 50 years can be attributed to "keeping its economy open, joining the fight against protectionism, building a world-class education system, investing in the skills of its workforce, in knowledge-based assets, in foreign economies through foreign direct investment, participating in the global value chains with highly efficient accompanying services".[6]

---

[2] Peter Borschberg, ed., *The Memoirs and Memorials of Jacques de Coutre: Security, Trade and Society in 16th- and 17th-century Southeast Asia* (Singapore: NUS Press, 2013).
[3] Borschberg, *Memoirs and Memorials*, 263.
[4] Borschberg, *Memoirs and Memorials*, 77.
[5] Chan Chin Bock, *Heart Work* (Singapore: Economic Development Board, 2002).
[6] Tommy Koh, Chang Li Lin and Joanna Koh, eds., *The Little Red Dot: Reflections of Foreign Ambassadors on Singapore* (Singapore: World Scientific, 2014), 13.

This inspiring success story has attracted people and business from all over the world. Belgians have not been immune to the lure of the city-state. One national describes the "charm of a tropical village" that first attracted him to Singapore. Some Belgians still feel nostalgic about what my immediate predecessor Roland Van Remoortele, writing in *Prestige* magazine, described as "the different smells, colours, sounds, shapes and sizes … all the things that made this island uniquely Singapore".

According to the old cliché, it is as truth universally acknowledged that those who come to Singapore and Singaporeans mostly care about money.

Even the *Congregatio Immaculati Cordis Mariae* (CICM — Congregation of the Immaculate Heart of Mary), the Scheut Missionaries, initially appear to have come to Singapore for financial reasons. Founded in 1865 by Father Theophile [Théophile or Theophiel] Verbist, a Belgian diocesan priest, the Congregation established a presence in Singapore in 1931. Although its main objective was to do mission work in China (the Singapore branch was originally set up as a "procure" to generate income), next to its China Outreach, it later engaged in pastoral work for migrants and seafarers and interreligious dialogue. Now based in Pandan Valley, its staff lives and works close to the people.

Today's Belgian residents in Singapore, in the words of Koen Cardon, are more likely to see the city-state as "the embodiment of globalisation and a multicultural society". The fate of Flanders Square reflects Singapore's evolution in this respect: in earlier days a "quaint" place with a (very) bad reputation, it is now part of a gentrified area with renovated shop houses and hipster coffee bars.

I would like to open a parenthesis here. Situated near Serangoon Road, Flanders Square is surrounded by streets with names that evoke the Great War: Kitchener Road, Somme Road, … Commemorating the war that started in 1914, the exhibition "The Great War in Broad Outlines", produced by the Belgian National Institute for Veterans and Victims of War, started its four-year world tour at Singapore's Changi Museum. On the occasion of the opening of the exhibition on 25 September 2014, museum director Jeya Ayadurai underlined its importance as "a reminder of how beautiful and fragile peace is and how not to take it for granted".

I close the parenthesis.

Singapore has become a global city with clear rules and a welcoming attitude to foreigners who want to set up a business. Koen Cardon, CEO for Asia of chemical logistics group Katoen Natie and vice-president of the Belgian Luxembourg Business Group, compares living in Singapore to being member of a golf club: "Golf is played on a green and well-tended field, where you need to adhere to many rules and regulations. Courtesy is most important and anyone who behaves well is most welcome to play." It is therefore no wonder that Singapore has been named seven times in a row the world's best place for doing business. Dirk Verbiest, former president of BLAS (Belgian and Luxembourg Association of Singapore), names the supportive attitude of the local authorities towards success as another factor attracting the more than 100 Belgian companies — big and small — that are currently based in Singapore. Some of them have quite recently finalised highly visible projects: Buzon has produced the supports that hold the deck on top of Marina Bay Sands, while Solvay opened its flagship Innovation Centre in Biopolis. Visibility was not one of the criteria for Vyncke to win the contract to build the biomass plant in Gardens by the Bay. On the contrary, the exhaust from their steam boiler had to remain unseen. Next time you visit the Gardens, try to guess which Super Tree hides the smokestack…

Belgian dredging companies such as Jan De Nul and DEME were responsible for a big chunk of the land reclamation that allowed Singapore to expand its territory by a whopping 20%. They contributed — and continue to contribute — quite literally to Singapore's development. Jurong Island, originally more than seven separate islets, offers a striking example. According to Chan Chin Bock, before developing the island as an integrated chemical hub, it proved necessary to study existing models in the US, Japan, Germany, the Netherlands… and Belgium.

DEME's area director Philip Hermans recalls the challenging conditions in which the work took place: "These islands were already completely built up with chemical plants, and the communication and logistics were done by boat [...] Also, pipelines transported chemicals between the different plants and some of these chemicals were very dangerous indeed. Our task was to fill up the sea between the islands according to a very stringent plan, without interrupting industrial production and with very limited access to the plants."

In its transition to a knowledge economy, Singapore continues its efforts to attract foreign talents (what Hercule Poirot, another famous Belgian, would call "the little grey cells"). Several Belgian researchers have answered the call. More than 10 years ago, Arnoud De Meyer was the founding dean of the INSEAD Asia Campus in Singapore. Today, he heads the Singapore Management University. Most Belgian universities have signed an exchange agreement with their Singapore counterparts. Many young Belgians have found their way to Singapore, spending a semester or more in this wonderful city. Each year, even more Singaporeans study at Belgian universities. These exchanges allow our young people to get to know each other, and to explore Southeast Asia and Europe respectively. The University of Antwerp and the National University of Singapore were the latest to sign a Memorandum of Understanding on closer scientific and academic cooperation.

More than 1,300 Belgian citizens have made Singapore their home. Fully one-third of them are children. Families have come to appreciate that there is more to Singapore than making a decent living. They enjoy what is on offer in leisure, arts, sports or check out the food scene.

Belgian artists are increasingly discovering Singapore as a budding art centre and as a hub to Asia. Singapore citizens these past few years got a taste of contemporary

Belgian dance with Sidi Larbi Cherkaoui, Compagnie Irene K. and — most recently at the Singapore International Festival of Arts — Miet Warlop. In the musical field, the Brussels Jazz Orchestra, Ozark Henry and Scala & the Kolacny Brothers all made their Asian debut in Singapore. The 2009 exhibition, "The Story of the Image: Old & New Masters from Antwerp", had a successful run in the National Museum of Singapore.

In 1968 Lee Kuan Yew could say that "poetry is a luxury we cannot afford". This holds no longer true. On the contrary, as the Red Pencil, a Singapore-based charity, demonstrates, art can serve as therapy, giving children who need it the ability to regain control of their lives. Laurence Vandenborre, its Belgian founder, adds: "when we rescue the child, we save the adult".

Last but not least, outside of Belgium, no country seems as "obsessed" with food as Singapore. Belgian cuisine is very much part of the incredibly varied local restaurant scene, with Gunther's and "Chef in Black" Emmanuel Stroobant having become household names. And Belgians, as well as Singaporeans, remember fondly the late entrepreneur Fabrice de Barsy who back in 1985 opened Singapore's first outdoor jazz-and-blues bar on Cuppage Terrace.

Singapore has known incredible growth over the past 50 years. Its leaders and people realise, however, that the city-state will face several challenges in the next half century: climate change, urbanisation, ageing, and so on. These challenges are not very different from those my country is facing. In November 2014, on the occasion of the Belgian Economic Mission to Singapore, led by Her Royal Highness Princess Astrid, we had the opportunity to exchange our experiences and expertise in these fields, with a particular emphasis on clean technologies and biomedical sciences. Belgium, like Singapore, offers innovative solutions to tomorrow's challenges. We therefore have a good basis for future win-win cooperation.

People-to-people contacts are expanding; trade between our countries is already very healthy. Singapore serves as a gateway to Asia; Belgium, with its geographic location, its connectivity and logistics and its highly productive labour force, is the perfect hub to Europe.

Prime Minister Lee Hsien Loong wants Singapore to be "a truly cosmopolitan city with an open and vibrant economy, where we work hard but enjoy a high quality of life". It holds all the cards to attain this goal. And I am confident that Belgians will want to help write this newest chapter of Singapore's (hi)story.

Happy anniversary, Singapore!

H.E. Gerard Cockx is the Belgian Ambassador to Singapore.

The Mermaid and the Merlion — 50 Years with Denmark and Singapore

Written by Mathilde Moyell Juul
(commissioned by the Royal Danish Embassy)

Petite, frail and easy to miss, the Little Mermaid in Copenhagen harbour is undoubtedly one of the most well-known symbols of Denmark. 10,000 km away, you'll find a sculpture six times the size of the Mermaid, also with a fishtail but with a majestic roaring lion head — the Singapore Merlion.

As was the case with the Mermaid, the Merlion was placed at the mouth of the city's river as a symbol to welcome all visitors. And when the statue was revealed to the public in 1972, Singapore's then Prime Minister, Lee Kuan Yew, stated that it was in fact the shy looking Danish Mermaid that served as inspiration to Singapore's new icon.

Singapore was and is inspired by Denmark for a reason. As with the two national symbols, the two countries are different, but share a lot of the same characteristics: Both are small nations with roughly the same population. Both are surrounded by water and large neighbours and dependent on external relations and trade. And both countries top international charts and often serve as each other's role models. However, today it isn't just the younger Singapore which looks to Denmark for inspiration, but these two countries benefit from one another's experiences and skills by collaborating on a wide array of topics. Although the official partnership goes back 50 years, the connection was made a lot earlier.

Disembarking for Singapore

The first Danish footprint on Singaporean soil was the first *Galathea* expedition, the purpose of which was to hand over existing colonies in India to the British and make an attempt to colonise the Nicobar Islands. The 26-month long journey also had a joint diplomatic, scientific and commercial purpose and the ship made its way to Singapore in 1846. To prepare for the arrival of *Galathea*, the first Danish consulate in Singapore was established in November 1845.

The East Asiatic Company [*Det Østasiatiske Kompagni*] set up a trading office in Singapore around the turn of the century. As industrialisation gathered pace during the 1960s and 1970s, Singapore became increasingly important as a trade hub. Jebsen & Jessen was the next significant Danish trading company to establish in Singapore in 1963, followed by Maersk in 1975. Subsequently, many more companies followed, and in 1989 the Danish government opened an embassy and appointed its first ambassador, Jørgen Peter Larsen.

The Early Years

During the 1980s, the small community of Danes living in Singapore amounted to about 40 people. One of them, Heine Askjær-Jensen, arrived in 1981 as a representative for Jebsen & Jessen and he remembers what life in Singapore was like back then:

"I arrived with my big atlas and that was all I knew about Singapore! As was the case with myself, Danish expatriates would typically represent a Danish company in sales or trade as part of a 1–2-man band. A working day would consist of reading letters, having lunch, replying to letters, perhaps a social event and then home," Heine Askjær-Jensen recalls. "Today the Danish expatriates either run the Danish offices or own their own companies out here, and being online 24 hours along with the rest of the world, the work day is a lot more stressful than when I first arrived," he says.

Spouses of Danish Expats

Being an accompanying spouse from overseas in the 1970s was also a lot different to what we see today, and finding or creating work for these spouses was tough. Following the initiative of Norwegian Marit Thome, the Scandinavian Society of Singapore (SSS) was established in 1975. Relaunched as the Scandinavian Women's Association (SWA) in 1995, the society served as an important social institution for spouses of Scandinavians working in Singapore. SWA filled a void and helped many Danish women to find a purpose through charitable work and by helping the local community. The first Danish president of SWA, Helle Wallevik, looks back at the early days of the society:

"SWA wasn't as well structured as it is today — we just forged ahead in an old fashioned pioneer-way. We arranged lots of coffee-mornings at the ambassador's residence or at my house where interesting people would speak, and we tried to find things to sell. One person knew where to get cheap sapphire jewellery at a good price (no one dared ask where from!), others made delicious cakes and some sold old books from their bookshelf. Quite a bit of money was scraped together, that primarily went to Singaporean families in need."

The aims and activities of the 40-year-old association have remained more or less the same. Today, 130 members benefit from the social aspect of the association, but helping local families is still the primary goal.

The Danish Seamen's Church

It wasn't just the Danish women who were in need of support when arriving in Singapore. The fast growing trade in the 1980s led to an increasing number of Danish ships and seamen disembarking the harbour in Singapore. Hence, the Danish Seamen's Church was founded in 1984 and based itself in a historical house on Mount Faber. The church quickly evolved as a meeting place for all Danes residing in Singapore, and the present chaplain, Kirsten Eistrup, believes that the longevity of the popularity of the church is due to it being a constant reminder of what it means to be Danish:

"The Seamen's Church becomes the place where it's visible what we are as Danes — culturally, nationally and also as Christians. In Singapore, the Danish church is a bearer and communicator of culture," she says.

Today, the church hosts a wide range of activities outside the services, including morning coffee, weekly Danish lunches, kids' playgroups, adults' workshops, concerts and keynote speakers.

The Danish Business Association

The social networks formed in the 1970s and 1980s were successful, but Danish business people were also eager to formalise a professional network that would actively contribute to business development and connections between Singapore and Denmark. This, however, proved to be a tough course. The Singaporean Chamber of Commerce was sceptical as they were worried about the topics to be discussed. But with the help of the Danish Chargé d'Affaires at the time, Kay R. D. Gad, the Danish Business Association of Singapore [DABS] was successfully established in 1983.

Heine Askjær-Jensen was one of the founders and took part in designing DABS's profile. "It shouldn't be a rich man's club, it was for everyone. An administrative body that could greet new Danish business people and create social events with interesting speakers," he recalls.

DABS was a success with noticeable events in the Danish-Singaporean society. Danish ministers came to speak and the Royal Danish Ballet was flown into Singapore to perform for the Danish expatriates. Today, the principles are the same, although the members are fewer due to the changing demands from Danish businesspeople and the multitude of other social and professional networks. However, the annual DABS charity ball is still very popular and the 30th anniversary ball in 2014 experienced the highest attendance rate in its history.

Business Grows

During the 1990s, the bilateral trade between Denmark and Singapore increased. More and more Danish companies were attracted to Singapore due to its strategic geographic location, making it a global transport and logistics hub as well as a regional financial center. Since then, business volume in Singapore has continued to grow, as Danish companies have gained access to not only Singapore, but also the fast-growing Southeast Asian market of more than 600 million people.

Today, 150 companies of Danish origin reside in Singapore and more than 1,500 Danish nationals live there. Many of them are employed in shipping companies, but Danish companies now represent a wide array of sectors: From renewable energy, food and medical to architecture and lifestyle products. Regardless of sector and size, Singapore is attractive for Danish companies, as it is known for being competitive and business friendly.

As a result, the shipping giant Maersk holds its largest fleet outside Denmark in Singapore. According to Managing Director, René Piil Pedersen, it is easy to attract employees and do business in Singapore: "The level of know-how is prominent and the international mindset makes it easy for us to do business. On top of that, Singapore is a safe place with no corruption, low crime rate and a very efficient system."

Not only mature companies enjoy the advantages of Singapore, however. Founded in Singapore 10 years ago, Norbreeze, a retail specialist, owes part of its success to the country's lucrative location and willingness to fund start-ups. Danish owner Anders Peter Juel Sauerberg says, "It has been essential for us to be based in Singapore because of the growth and expansion opportunities in Southeast Asia. It's easy to set up a company here, and from day one, the government has supported us, not only financially, but with various aids that have helped the company grow in the right direction."

Mutual Learning

The political goodwill to nurture and strengthen the partnership between Denmark and Singapore has resulted in a number of strategic cooperation agreements, most recently within the water industry in 2014 and the maritime industry in 2012.

At the signing of the maritime agreement in 2012, Ole Sohn, the Danish Minister of Business and Growth at the time, recalled, "Denmark and Singapore have high quality ship registers. Just as Singapore is the maritime hub of Asia, it is my ambition to lead Denmark to hold a similar position in Europe." The maritime ties were equally strengthened in 2014 by the collaboration between Copenhagen

Business School and Singapore Management University, aiming at developing skilled industry talent through private sector and industry involvement as well as international exchange programmes.

Historically, the close link between Denmark and Singapore has been shipping and trade, as maritime activities account for as much as 40 % of Danish-Singaporean business. However, the countries have a number of other mutual interests, according to Denmark's current ambassador to Singapore, Berit Basse. "Today, the exchange of experience happens within many areas including innovation, education and welfare solutions as well as developing inclusive and liveable cities," she says.

Singapore has a particular interest in the Danish cycling culture, so much that Prime Minister Lee Hsien Loong recently mentioned Denmark as a role model in a speech on Singapore's future initiatives on becoming a clean and green nation. He said, "If the Danes can cycle in the winter, we should be able to do the same in the tropics."

Denmark is equally inspired by Singapore's concepts for a green and smart nation, intelligent transport systems as well as the country's long-term master plan for growth and development. Frequent visits by ministers or official delegations go both ways, as well as an increasing number of tourists contributing to a closer relationship between the two countries.

The Future

Singapore's openness to talent, ideas and people is one of the reasons why Danes came to Singapore and still do. Singapore is an attractive country for Danish individuals, families and companies, as the country is safe, efficient, low on corruption, based on diversity and internationally oriented.

According to Ambassador Berit Basse, the results that Singapore has achieved during the past 50 years are impressive. "One of Singapore's strengths is the ability to constantly be outward and forward-looking and to execute the best ideas in their own way", she says, while foreseeing a future of mutual learning on an even higher scale. "As Denmark and Singapore are both international frontrunners in many similar areas, I see great potential for an even closer partnership in order to benefit from each other's strengths and experience."

Ever since Denmark tied a formal knot with Singapore back in 1965 and the then Prime Minister revealed the now iconic Merlion a couple of years later, the ties between the countries have only grown stronger. Along with Singapore's impressive development, Denmark is now looking to the East for inspiration and trade. 50 years have passed; the Mermaid and the Merlion still stand to greet visitors to their small and strong nations, but are also reminders of how inspiration and ideas have developed into a solid lasting partnership between the wise and inventive nation up North and the fresh, fast-paced island out East.

Preserving the Excellent Connection between Finland and Singapore through the Young Generation

Tuukka Väisänen

Excellent ties between Finland and Singapore date back to the beginning of Singapore's path as a sovereign nation. Since then, the ties have been gradually blossoming and started blooming in 1990s. Both countries, of course, are small by population and there are many other countries which are more significant partners to them. Nevertheless, even with the small populations and their geographical locations almost 10,000 km apart, ties can be described as excellent. In this essay I will reflect on how these excellent ties can be preserved as the generations change, and which topics might be the new shared areas of interest between Singapore and Finland.

Economic ties between Finland and Singapore can be characterised as reasonably tight and economic activity is vivid, but more importantly rich in opportunities. There are many areas of cooperation underway and even more in the planning stage. Besides more traditional prominent fields which include, for example, healthcare and education, one possible area of cooperation and shared interest is the start-up enterprise sector which is slowly challenging the more traditional industries, at least in terms of publicity and hype, but also due to structural change taking place in many advanced economies. Especially, start-ups in the technology sector are becoming more prevalent all around the world due to ever-growing importance of all types of electronic gadgets and increased accessibility to devices and internet even in poorer countries. There are a number of clusters, so-called hubs, in the world of which Silicon Valley is definitely the most influential by a great margin. On the European scale, Helsinki's recent success as a global city has unquestionably shaken the mindsets of Finns and created new hope amid the extending economic recession.

The entrepreneurial start-up boom in Finland is very recent. To a great extent, it has been concretely created by young students, and this is due to a range of reasons, among them the end of the Nokia era in Finland. Nokia used to account for a great deal of the Finnish GDP, and consequently the whole nation was too dependent on the company, at least emotionally. Nokia used to be the dream company for many university graduates, and practically none was interested in an entrepreneurial career which was regarded as some kind of a failure those days. Many thought it was only for people who were not able to secure a "real job". Furthermore, in the mid-2000s, an idea of a multidisciplinary university became alive in Finland. It was realised in 2010 when Aalto University, a merger of top Finnish universities, Helsinki University of Technology, Helsinki School of Economics, and University of Art and Design Helsinki, started operations. The coincidental timing of these two, and some other factors, led to rapid development that had never been seen in Finland.

Concretely, things started to evolve when an individual student from the former Helsinki School of Economics experienced a "eureka moment" while visiting the campus of the Massachusetts Institute of Technology (MIT) during an economics club's excursion to Boston. He was seriously impressed by the atmosphere at MIT when it comes to entrepreneurial spirit. In contrast to Finland, entrepreneurs at MIT were treated like rock stars and heroes, and many top students wanted to become entrepreneurs instead of choosing a more typical investment banking or consulting career, for example. Once this gentleman returned to Finland, he set up an entrepreneurship society named Aalto Entrepreneurship Society for the students of the forthcoming Aalto University.

At the beginning, everything was really small-scale and events were small with people talking to each other about entrepreneurship and just pitching ideas to a bunch of interested listeners. The university supported the initiatives by providing the space, for instance. The reception was positive since the idea supported the core mission of the university: bringing technology, business and design together. Now, a few years later, the Aalto Entrepreneurship Society has sparked many by-products, seeding accelerator programmes, internship programmes including a programme sending young bright students to work in Silicon Valley, and last but not least, a start-up conference, Slush, bringing more than 10,000 visitors and more than a thousand new companies and big venture capital investors to rainy and dark Helsinki in November every year. The event, the CEO of which is a 25-year-old student, has become the target of interest of many influential persons around the world recently. Thus, things have changed in the past 10 years. Recently, these "entrepreneurial societies" have been established in connection with many major Finnish universities.

Singapore is fast becoming a sort of start-up hub as well and its efforts have not gone unnoticed in Europe. The business friendly environment, low taxation, educated people and efforts to boost innovation make it an ideal location for start-ups, especially to those aiming for fast growth in Asian markets. The universities in Singapore, such as NUS and NTU, are world-class and their quality surpasses the Finnish universities on average. NUS has even established overseas colleges in the US, China and Sweden with the aim of fostering entrepreneurship. What then prevents Singapore from becoming another Silicon Valley, when the premises to run a new company are outstanding, and there are plenty of high net worth investors in the region?

It may be the same case as it was in Finland a decade ago. People want and expect a secure career, and failure is frowned upon. Especially, when tuition fees of tertiary education are high, choosing a financially secure path is lucrative. Mindsets in Finland have changed; they can change in Singapore too. What if the cooperation that already exists on the level of student exchange at the universities, would also be implemented on this level? These "entrepreneur societies", though independent, are often closely linked to their respective universities. It does not take many additional steps, and there are plenty of best practices to learn from each other. On the bigger picture, Finland can learn how to create an environment where business could thrive, whereas Singapore could in turn study how to use its current resources to make innovation flourish.

Compared to previous generations who had far less opportunities to travel and go on exchange programmes, today's generations and future ones can preserve the strong people-to-people connections between our countries also through our travels and studies. Speaking from the Finnish point of view, I actually consider traveling as one of the focal connection points of younger Finns to Singapore. Both for leisure and studies, Singapore is really popular among Finnish university students as an exchange destination; it is exotic, warm and far away, but at the same time really safe with high standards of living. Later on, these people will enter business life and always have Singapore in their heart. It also works the opposite way, as young Singaporeans are encouraged to go on exchange and the Nordic countries, including Finland, have been popular destinations for many young Singaporeans. This development is truly beneficial for both sides.

The daily direct flight connection between Helsinki and Singapore has increased Singapore's visibility in Finland. Southeast Asia is a popular region especially among the independent, born-global generation of under-35s, and many come to the region for a mixture of city and beach holiday. Bangkok used to be the entry point for many, but as the security situation in Thailand has had its ups and downs, Finns have started to flock to Singapore. Instead of just being a necessary transit point on the way to Australia, it has become a holiday destination of its own, and for good reasons.

Also at the same time, more Singaporean tourists can be seen on the snowy streets of Helsinki. Finland may not have the appeal of some great European nations with their grand capitals full of history, but is still an exotic destination which has not yet been spoiled by mass tourism. What sets Finland apart from its most European counterparts is the distinct culture and untouched nature with true wilderness. For many Asians however, Finland is only seen from the airport transit area window when transferring to a connection heading for other European cities. The beautiful nature would be one of the selling points for them to stay for a bit longer. Iceland, for example, has marketed very well the possibility of having free stopovers on the way between Europe and North America with their flag carrier, and many people end up visiting Iceland this way.

Singapore is celebrating its 50th anniversary in 2015. Finland as an independent nation is turning 100 years old in 2017. These are really big celebrations, marking a significant milestone in both countries. What unites us is that we are young societies which have previously been controlled by someone else, and our identities are still developing. We both have however come far from where we started, and left our footprints on this world. Our roles might be different in the future world order, and thus, it will be interesting to see what the future brings us. Hopefully, it includes ever-strengthening cooperation between Finland and Singapore.

Tuukka Väisänen is currently finishing his postgraduate studies in Finland in the field of finance. He recently spent a three-month period at the Embassy of Finland in Singapore, where he got the opportunity to deepen his knowledge about the Southeast Asian countries, their economic profiles and politics.

Cultural and Scientific Cooperation between Italy and Singapore

Contribution from the Embassy of Italy and Italian Cultural Institute

Since the birth of the Republic of Singapore, Italy has built and maintained strong and friendly ties with the city-state.

Several noteworthy exchanges in the fields of Art, Music, Education and Science between Italy and Singapore have taken place in the past three decades with the establishment of the Italian Cultural Institute in Singapore, enriching the diverse and vibrant cultural life in the Lion City.

The Italian Cultural Institute

The Italian Cultural Institute (ICI) was established in 1989 and for the past 26 years it has acted as a cultural gateway and a lively go-between between Italy and Singapore not only promoting Italian language and culture but acting as a clearing house for comprehensive information about Italy at large, its schools, academies, and universities.

Since its inception, the ICI has striven to bring to Singapore the best of Italian music, art, cinema, design, and theatre. Throughout the years, several prominent Italian cultural events have taken place with the collaboration or through the organisation of the Italian Cultural Institute, such as the memorable concert by "I Solisti Veneti" in 1998 followed by the renowned orchestra of the Accademia di Santa Cecilia in 2000. The Baroque Italian Chamber Orchestra "I Musici" made its debut in Singapore in 2011 and returned to the Lion City in 2013. Italy's most prominent violinist, Maestro Uto Ughi, came for the first time to Singapore in 2000 and, on the occasion of Singapore's 50th Jubilee, was back in March 2015 for another magnificent concert at the newly restored Victoria Concert Hall.

In the field of cinema, the Institute, in collaboration with the National Museum of Singapore, organised unique film retrospectives in 2008 (Michelangelo Antonioni) and in 2010 (Federico Fellini) that were extremely well received. For the past 12 years, the Institute has been organising the annual "Italian Film Festival", in collaboration with the Singapore Film Society, to present the most contemporary movies as well as a selection of beloved classics.

In 2005, the extraordinary exhibition of the "Musei Vaticani" or Vatican Museums made headlines and provided Singaporeans with an opportunity to enjoy a selection of Italian masterpieces. Again, in 2010 the large exhibition on "Pompeii: Life in a Roman Village 79 CE" attracted thousands of interested spectators to the National Museum. In 2014 and into 2015, an exclusive thematic exhibition at the ArtScience Museum is presenting Leonardo da Vinci's legacy and has brought for the first time to Singapore original drawings and sketches of the great Renaissance Man.

Italy, through its Embassy and its Cultural Institute is always thrilled to participate in Singapore's Festivals. One, in particular, the Singapore International Photography Festival, from its very beginning in 2008, has featured a steady number of prominent Italian photographers selected and invited to Singapore by its curators. In 2006, it is noteworthy to mention that the Arts House and the Italian cultural Institute organised a collective of three of Italy most acclaimed contemporary photographers: Franco Fontana, Giovanni Gastel and Ferdinando Scianna.

The Singapore International Guitar Festival, launched more than 10 years ago, has featured annually Italian guitarists, both classic and "finger style" virtuosos.

In the field of Fashion, we can mention the memorable retrospective on the iconic Italian designer Valentino in 2006; more recently, the exhibition on the "60 years of Italian Fashion" was organised in collaboration with Singaporean Partners, the Italian Trade Commission and the Italian Cultural Institute, confirming the ongoing interest of Singaporeans in Italian brands and fashion.

The Bilateral Agreement on Cultural and Scientific Cooperation

The Bilateral Agreement on Cultural and Scientific Cooperation between Italy and Singapore provides a strong basis to enhance cultural, academic, and scientific ties between the two countries.

In the past 10 years, Italian universities and colleges have received more than 500 enrolments from Singaporean students who participated in exchange programmes or have completed and graduated from universities and higher education institutions. The same can be said about Italian students attending Singaporean universities, confirming a growing trend of student exchanges between our two countries. Over the last few years, 37 Singaporean students have gone on Italian Government-sponsored scholarships to study in Italian universities. It is clear that exchange programmes between Italian universities and the four major universities in the city-state present a significant and growing trend.

More than 80 Italian researchers and scientists work in Singapore's main scientific hubs, such as A*STAR, as well as at all major universities and in the private sector.

Several Memoranda of Understanding and Inter-University Agreements have being signed between Italian and Singaporean universities and colleges and the number has been growing steadily in the past three years, the last one being an important MoU between the Universita' Politecnico in Milan and the National University of Singapore to enhance exchanges and joint research in the field of Design, IT and Electronics.

The Italian Language in Singapore

Since the inauguration of the Italian Cultural Institute and the launch of the first School of Italian Language in Singapore, an average of 360 Singaporean students have attended Italian classes each year. Over the years since, the ICI has taught Italian to more than 7,000 Singaporeans, several of them reaching proficient level and sitting the final Italian Certification Exams.

In 2012, the Nanyang Technological University introduced Italian courses in its faculty of Humanities thanks to a special Italian Government Grant, making NTU the first university in Singapore to teach Italian at the university level.

Concluding Remarks

2015 marks 50 years of Singapore's independence as well as of Italy and Singapore's bilateral relations which started on 28 October 1965. Mutual interest in each other, from culture to finance to trade, is as strong as ever and we are confident we will see the further flourishing of all these ties.

Singapore and Luxembourg: Small Partners, Big Visions!

Contribution from the Luxembourg Embassy

At first sight it is hard to identify the connections between Singapore and Luxembourg. And it does not become much easier at second sight.

There are no direct air connections between Singapore and Luxembourg; you would have to transfer at least once to reach either destination, unless of course you were a piece of cargo transported by Luxembourg's all-cargo airline, one of Europe's biggest, on one of its many direct flights to Singapore.

There are no obvious maritime links either. Singapore has developed, and continues to develop its harbour to cement its position as a major regional logistics hub. Luxembourg is a land-locked country. One could argue that the Moselle flows into the Atlantic Ocean (thus correcting the misperception that the Moselle flows into the Rhine) and that all oceans are connected. But this link is rather tenuous.

Yet, there exists a kindred spirit between Singapore and Luxembourg. A way of thinking that has been shaped by the geographical realities and the challenges of their respective neighbourhoods. Singaporeans and Luxembourgers are conscious of the relative size of their countries and have thus developed an essentially international outlook. After all, it is easier to see beyond your borders if those borders are so close.

Trade for Singaporeans and Luxembourgers always meant trade with foreigners and the wider world, looking beyond the confines of our respective national markets to achieve economies of scale. The reliance on trade and the limited means at our disposal to defend our interests by military force also explain why Singapore and Luxembourg have always been such staunch supporters of international law. Our attachment to the rule of law has also contributed to our success as centres of international finance and banking.

Luxembourg had independence thrust upon it when the Great European Powers decided in the 19th century to divide the Kingdom of the Netherlands into three constituent parts, the Netherlands, Belgium and Luxembourg. Luxembourg continued to be coveted by its neighbours following its independence. The disasters of World Wars I and II convinced our leaders that peaceful cooperation and the common exploitation of economic resources would be the only solution to overcome the divisions in Europe in a sustainable way.

Singapore in turn had independence thrust upon it when the Malaysian Federation and Singapore decided to part ways 50 years ago.

Luxembourg and Singapore are both, to use an image employed by Lee Kuan Yew, small fish swimming in a pond together with much larger fish.

Luxembourg established an economic union with Belgium in 1922 already, which became in many ways a forerunner of the European Economic Community (EEC), of which Luxembourg was a founding member, and the European Union. The common Belgian and Luxembourgish Franc was replaced by the common European currency, the euro, on 1 January 1999.

After separation from the Malaysian Federation, Singapore was left to fend for itself but invested a great amount of energy in support for the progress of the Association of Southeast Asian Nations (ASEAN) as a means to foster regional cooperation in the economic, social, cultural, technical, educational and other fields. Two years after Singapore became independent, the document establishing ASEAN was signed by its founding members Indonesia, the Philippines, Malaysia, Singapore and Thailand in Bangkok on 8 August 1967.

Singapore and Luxembourg unfortunately have always had limited resources, but fortunately we both had leaders with a vision and an ambition not to be daunted by these limitations. Singapore has been able to rely on its strategic location for world trade and its harbour as a backbone on which to build its economy. Luxembourg on the other hand has been able to rely on its location in the heart of Europe and was fortunate enough to benefit from substantial iron ore reserves, the exploitation of which kick-started the modern Luxembourg economy, and which brought it into the European Coal and Steel Community, a forerunner of the EEC. Fortunately for Singapore, the harbour is still developing while Luxembourg's iron ore and the corresponding steel industry have long been on the wane.

Luxembourg and Singapore have always been aware of the necessity to diversify their economies and establish activities of economic excellence that could compete in their respective regions and beyond. One of the areas into which Singapore and Luxembourg have diversified, in a very successful way, is international finance and banking. The international financial centres of Singapore and Luxembourg are now sometimes competing on the global market but the development of Singapore and Luxembourg as financial centres was also the result of the collaboration of the different actors at all levels of these centres: from the politicians with or without governmental responsibilities to the officials from the Monetary Authority of Singapore (MAS) and the Monetary Institute of Luxembourg (IML), the different banking associations and organisations and the financial institutions and banks.

In order to remain competitive in their regions and in an ever more integrated international market, Singapore and Luxembourg need to continue to innovate, maintain and increase their competitiveness and invest in the education of their workforces or create the conditions to attract the best from abroad. The wealth we managed to create in our respective countries has benefitted not only our citizens but also foreign residents, which represent a significant percentage of those residing in Luxembourg and in Singapore. The wealth we created in Luxembourg and Singapore also benefitted those residing across our borders. Nearly 180,000 people from Belgium, France and Germany cross the border each day to work in Luxembourg whilst more than 300,000 commute daily from Malaysia to work in Singapore.

The economic influence of Luxembourg and Singapore thus extends well beyond the borders of our respective countries. Politically as well, Luxembourg and Singapore punch well above their weight. Luxembourg, a founding member of the United Nations, has just completed its first tenure at the UN Security Council and has earned plaudits for the competent way it handled international issues, such as children in armed conflict. Luxembourg, a founding member of the European Communities has managed to play a role well beyond its size in European affairs because its leaders have always acted as honest brokers in order to facilitate understanding between the main actors in Europe.

Singapore has likewise been a motor in moving things forward in ASEAN and it will look proudly upon the impending establishment of the ASEAN Economic Community by the end of 2015. Singapore has also been a successful contributor and participant at the G20 meetings. It is a credit to the competence of its leaders and the excellence of its diplomacy that Singapore, a country of 5.5 million inhabitants, manages to be invited regularly to attend the G20 meetings and to exert a constructive influence on its discussions.

In spite of their respective sizes, Singapore and Luxembourg have earned the respect of their regional and international partners and we will continue to work towards this end.

Singapore and the Netherlands: Building the Future Together

Katrijn de Ronde, Embassy of the Kingdom of the Netherlands

In 1930 Karl Willem Benjamin van Kleef, a Dutchman living in the city of Haarlem, left his entire estate to the Municipal Government of Singapore. He left Singapore S$160,000 (current value almost S$9 million).

The reasons for his bequest remain shrouded in mystery. Born in Batavia, mining expert Van Kleef moved to Singapore where he ran a successful business. In 1913, he finally left Singapore to go back to the Netherlands. His wish was for his inheritance to be used for the "embellishment of Singapore Town". The Municipal Government of Singapore decided to build an aquarium named after its benefactor. It was, according to the Singapore National Archives, the first of its kind in Southeast Asia: "a modern, forward looking aquarium which exemplified the progressive direction the country itself aspired to".

Progress waits for no man, and the aquarium closed its doors in 1999. But the name Van Kleef lives on in Singapore as the Van Kleef Aquatic Science Centre, a world-class research facility on all things hydro.

This is a story of the Netherlands and Singapore. It is a story of strong business relationships and intertwining economic growth. It is a story of two nations, across the globe, which recognised a kindred spirit in each other. Two nations that struggled to carve out a place for themselves in the face of great difficulties, and two nations that thrive through embracing learning, acting responsibly, building on the past and looking to the future.

From the Past to the Future

Technology company, Royal Philips is perhaps the best-known Dutch brand for consumers in Singapore. "Philips' development here closely follows Singapore's own economic growth," says Harjit Gill, CEO of Philips ASEAN & Pacific. Singapore started out as a place for low-end manufacturing, upgraded to high-value manufacturing and is now moving into Research and Development (R&D) and Innovation.

Philips' history mirrors this development. It started its trading office in Singapore in 1951 and grew to become a subsidiary with manufacturing activities in the 1960s. By the seventies, Singapore had become one of the world's largest manufacturing centres for Philips. In the 1980s and 1990s, Philips' activities evolved to include design, product development and high value manufacturing as the company focused more on technology transfer and collaboration. Today, Singapore is the regional headquarters for Philips in the Asia Pacific and has R&D and Innovation activities which will ramp up with its new headquarters facility in 2016.

Ms. Gill has worked in Singapore three times over the years and has witnessed many of the changes in Singapore and in Philips. She said, "I first lived in Singapore from 1993 to 1996. Those were exciting days as the country was developing rapidly and diversifying its economic structure, hosting a wide range of businesses and activities. The mindset was straightforward and very much about 'getting it done'."

Other companies see the same development. Ruud Keesom of Gouda-based Delta Marine Consultants, which celebrated its 25th anniversary in Singapore in 2014 and employs 25 people, says, "Singapore is moving to the high end of the value chain with integrated solutions and complex projects. Ten years ago, there might still have been 'cheap engineering', but that is now moving to neighbouring countries." Dr. Michael Bolt, Director of NXP's Research Asia Lab, agrees, "It is already happening. The R&D activities in Singapore, compared to the region, are phenomenal."

Sustainable business is an important part of this shift, Dutch companies note. Only by being sustainable does a company ensure long-term growth and profitability. This refers to more than just the environment: it is a mindset to build with an eye to the future. Paul Forschelen, regional business manager at Boskalis International (a leading maritime services company), says: "The joint venture between Keppel and Smit [a subsidiary of Boskalis, ed.] is 27 years old and still going strong. That is a clear indication of the level of trust and appreciation on both sides."

Grand Old Companies

Philips, Boskalis, DMC and NXP build on a longstanding tradition of Dutch business in Singapore. The Dutch have settled in and around Singapore, bringing business and trade connections, for more than a hundred years. Many of those early arrivals are still around. Take private banking establishment ABN Amro bank, arriving in Singapore in 1858 as the Netherlands Trading Society and now the oldest, still existing bank in the Lion City. Another is mining firm Billiton, which shipped its tin from Indonesia to Singapore for smelting and which has grown into world-leading miner BHP Billiton. BHP Billiton's current office at the top of Marina Bay Financial Centre affords a luxurious view of Royal Dutch Shell's impressive refinery and chemicals hub across Bukom and Jurong Islands, first founded in 1891, tying the two centenaries together.

Grand old companies like these have been crucial in creating ecosystems, as can be seen in the port where large players like Boskalis, Van Oord and Damen's shipyard are accompanied by SME suppliers like Hatenboer Water, Trustlube and IMT. Well-known and longstanding multinationals like dairy company FrieslandCampina and producer of paints, coatings and specialty chemicals AkzoNobel pave the way for smaller and niche-focused companies to enter the Singapore market.

Albert Winsemius

Although Karl van Kleef left his entire estate to Singapore, it is undoubtedly Dutchman Albert Winsemius who gave Singapore the greatest legacy. He arrived in 1960 with a team of the United Nations Programme for Technical Assistance to do a feasibility survey for industrial expansion in Singapore and he was Singapore's chief economic adviser for the next 24 years.

Winsemius' first report painted a grim picture of a place rife with riots and strikes, but also a place of distinct possibility. He worked closely with the Singapore government to put into place the conditions for economic growth.

Albert Winsemius was no stranger to this work — in fact, he had done much the same thing for his native country as a financial adviser to the Dutch section of the Marshall Plan (the US aid "Europe Recovery Plan" after the WWII). This too has been a resounding economic success, propelling the Netherlands from war-ravaged ruins to its current strong global position.

It was Mr. Winsemius who championed the idea of attracting global companies to create trust in the Singapore economy and build a business ecosystem of profitable small, medium and large enterprises. He personally convinced Philips and Shell to invest in Singapore in the sixties. But that was only the beginning. Mr. Winsemius believed in sustainable growth and placed great emphasis on learning: "We must upgrade cheap labour to quality. We only have hands and brains. If we want to develop, we must train our hands and brains to be skilled."

Collaboration and Open Innovation

When Ms. Harjit Gill returned to Singapore in 2006, the country had already bounced back from the Asian economic crisis. Ms. Gill says, "There was a completely different landscape of companies and activities. There were many R&D

activities in new industries like clean technology, and the social and arts scene was much more vibrant than in the nineties."

As Philips is becoming a company focused on healthtech and sustainable lighting solutions, Ms. Gill sees a lot of synergy with Singapore's goals to become a smart city and Living Lab to create and test-bed innovations for the region.

She says, "At Philips, we aim to help reshape and optimise population health management by leveraging big data and delivering care from hospital to home. We see lots of opportunities to tap into the ecosystem of public and private companies in Singapore to collaborate and co-create locally relevant innovations that address people's needs and solve societal challenges such as healthcare for an aging population."

Open innovation and collaboration are where Ms. Gill sees Philips and Singapore heading in the future. In the Netherlands, Philips's former laboratory in Eindhoven now hosts over 130 companies and knowledge institutions which share R&D facilities. In Singapore, Philips is working with Eastern Health Alliance and Changi General Hospital to pilot Singapore's first telehealth program to monitor the health of heart patients. According to Ms. Gill, "Singapore continues to be a key regional innovation hub for Philips. Over the years, it has built strong capabilities and an ecosystem that supports open innovation. This is important as no one company has the solution to solve the complex challenges we face today, especially in healthcare where there are many stakeholders in the care cycle."

"The Philips culture is at heart very much like the Dutch culture," says Ms. Gill. "There is an openness to innovation, a willingness to take risks but always calculated risks, and a strong belief in sustainability. I find that this resonates very well with Singaporeans who want to learn and are driven."

Maritime Ecosystem

"Theoretically, one day, there should be enough ports and harbours," says Mr. Paul Forschelen of maritime company Boskalis, world leaders in dredging and land reclamation. "But in practice, that hasn't happened yet." Boskalis arrived in Singapore in the mid-1980s. Since then, it has grown to a company with over a 1,000 employees, easily the largest yard and office after the Dutch home base. "It surprised me too," says Mr. Forschelen. "But it does show the importance of Singapore as a hub for business."

Both Singapore and the Netherlands are logistical hubs in their respective region, Southeast Asia and Europe. The ties between the ports of Singapore and Rotterdam are strong, and many companies meet each other on both sides of the world. Dutch companies Boskalis, DMC and Vopak, the world's largest independent tank storage provider, are in Singapore, and Singapore companies such as Keppel and Franklin Offshore have a presence in Rotterdam. Although trade between the two ports has historically been strong, the boom came in the 1980s with Singapore's expansion. Singapore is among the largest container ports in the world, and has a thriving ecosystem around all things maritime, including, for instance, AkzoNobel's global headquarters for its marine paints and coatings business.

"This is a floating restaurant," says Mr. Ruud Keesom, Managing Director of Delta Marine Consultants as he points to a picture of restaurant Catalunya at Marina Bay. "It's the one of the few restaurants in the world that has a custom built floating device."

Engineering firm DMC has seen the shift to high end engineering since its arrival in the 1980s. "We are not necessarily competing on price, but we are adding value by offering innovative and integrated solutions." And in order to be able to do that, DMC itself is investing in its Singapore office: "DMC is looking to develop two global office hubs, one in the Netherlands and one in Singapore, with an interchangeable level of knowledge and expertise to service the respective markets." Because, as Mr. Keesom stresses, Singapore is the place to be, now and in the future: "It's unique to have all global players gathered together into one place as in Singapore. We have slowly built our reputation here, and we have a strong track record. An ecosystem such as this is not copied easily."

Vision of the Future

Listening to Dr. Bolt of NXP Research Asia Lab, it seems as if the future has already arrived, in the shape of the internet of things and near field sensors. Singapore has presented ambitious plans to become a smart city. It is a future of which the Dutch look forward to be part, as collaborators and contributors of specialised knowledge. One of these companies is NXP, with its emphasis on "secure connections for a smarter world". In 2013 solar car Stella rode Singapore's streets, guided in part by NXP's chip technology.

But a completely self-driving car is still a "long-term goal", Dr. Bolt cautions. As the director of Research NXP Asia Lab, he works closely with educational institutions but also with other stakeholders, such as SMEs to find innovative solutions.

"The government is pushing hard for a knowledge economy and they are well placed to do so", Dr. Bolt says. A knowledge economy, he explains, is an economy that is always building and progressing, not necessarily through major breakthroughs, but by incremental innovation. It is also an economy where, in the face of economic change, people can be taught new skills and re-enter the work force. "By that standard, the Netherlands is already a knowledge economy," he says. Singapore too is showing hallmark traits of such a system: "Singapore has outmanoeuvred cheaper competition before, by going upscale. Just look at shipping." He also points to the Singapore University of Technology and Design as another sign of the future: "Singapore is taking a risk with a different education system. They are trying to adapt — but they are starting with the academically strong."

Singapore and the Netherlands

In 1931, two men walked into the bar at Raffles Hotel, had a drink and started a beer company. They named their brew "Tiger Beer". The company brought into being by this chance meeting, was a joint venture by Fraser and Neave and Dutch Heineken.

Even though the beginning may be small, the enduring relationship has proved sturdy. Companies and countries have grown together. Tiger beer is currently brewed in nine countries and available in over 70 countries globally.

Sustainability is the key to enduring good business. It is no coincidence that AkzoNobel's Singapore R&D lab developed an innovative paint that can lower a buildings' energy use by as much as 10%.

Dr. Bolt of NXP admires Singapore's capacity for re-invention: "Singapore is very careful in changing. But in saying that, there is the willingness to let everything be up for change." And so the country has been a natural fit for Dutch multinationals, who too dare to take decisive action.

"We are building the future here," says Ms. Harjit Gill, talking about Philips' plans to build a new regional facility in Singapore which will house new R&D, co-creation and tele-health activities to drive the company's innovations for the region. "We want to contribute to building Singapore's next 50 years."

Polish People in Singapore: The Foundation of Strong Singapore-Poland Relations

Zenon Kosiniak-Kamysz and Katarzyna Kryczka

It is impressive to see the list of events, publications and festivities that Singapore is scheduling in celebration of its 50th anniversary of independence. The illustrious golden jubilee of Singapore is one of the reasons why influential travel guide *Lonely Planet* names Singapore as one of the world's top places to visit in 2015. The Lion City will certainly not fail to impress. This special occasion moves hearts and stirs minds of Singaporeans and Singapore's friends from around the world.

On the occasion, it is an honour and a pleasure to be contributing to this festive publication, which takes a look at Singapore's links and ties with countries of Europe. We would like to thank Dr. Yeo Lay Hwee, the Director of the EU Centre, for this opportunity.

Looking back at the last 50 years, Singaporeans have many reasons to celebrate and plenty of achievements to be proud of. In the course of just one generation, the Little Red Dot, as it is famously referred to, grew to become, among other things, a modern metropolis and a global business centre. Singapore's success is acknowledged worldwide and Singaporeans have earned the respect and admiration of the world for their resilience and extraordinary achievements. Such recognition resonates strongly also in faraway Poland. When the current Minister of Foreign Affairs of Poland, Grzegorz Schetyna assumed office in late 2014, he referred to Singapore in his inaugural speech as among the selected countries with which Poland would like to extend and deepen bilateral ties. At first glance, this connection might seem somewhat unlikely; in fact, it is not. In line with Polish diplomacy mission "to serve Poland, to build Europe, to understand the world" comprehending Singapore and its unique story makes a noteworthy part of understanding the world.

Historically, trade ties between the Polish state and independent Singapore date back to the early days of Singapore's statehood. In May 1966 Prime Minister Lee Kuan Yew, Minister for Foreign Affairs S. Rajaratnam and Minister for Social Affairs Othman Wok paid a visit to Poland, then celebrating 1,000 years of its history. As a result, a reciprocal "most favoured nation" trade treaty was concluded later the same year. In 1969 diplomatic relations was established.

However, it was only after Poland broke away from communist rule and transformed into a modern democracy and a market economy that exchanges between two countries intensified considerably. In the beginning of the century, Prime Minister Goh Chok Tong's official trip to Poland in 2001 was followed by a series of the highest-level visits from Poland to Singapore. Poland's foreign minister Włodzimierz Cimoszewicz was on an official state visit to Singapore in 2002, Prime Minister Leszek Miller in 2003, President Aleksander Kwaśniewski in 2004 and Prime Minister Marek Belka in 2005. Amidst the visits, the first resident Polish Ambassador to Singapore assumed office in 2004. The office of the Polish Embassy in Wisma Atria, at the heart of Orchard Road, became a piece of Poland in Singapore.

With Poland's accession to the European Union in 2004, there were more opportunities for political dialogue at the highest level and for closer cooperation. Although leadership changes in Poland prevented Prime Minister's Lee Hsien Loong's trip planned in 2007, he met his Polish counterpart Donald Tusk a year later at the sidelines of the 7th ASEM Summit in Beijing. In culmination of bilateral ties after that meeting, Mr. Tusk embarked on an official visit to Singapore in November 2012 and Singapore's Prime Minister reciprocated the visit a year later in October 2013. To get a measure of Poland's interest in fostering bilateral ties with Singapore, we might consider that in the last 15 years there have been more highest-level state visits to Singapore than to Canada — a country much larger by size and population with a Polish community of almost a million people.

Besides the ever stronger official relations, the story of the Polish people whose lives and livelihoods are interwoven with Singapore is a less documented, yet no less fascinating facet of the contacts between Singapore and Poland. It so appears that Polish people have been coming to Singapore since its early days, for travel, for work or for love. In a way, Poland has always been here in small bits and pieces. Some lasting legacy thereof is worth mentioning in the anniversary year.

Perhaps the most famous for having found a place in the world's literature are the stints in Singapore by Joseph Conrad, as the Polish-born writer Józef Konrad Korzeniowski is known to the world. A son of a Polish nobleman, Joseph Conrad, the sailor and famous English-language writer, stayed in Singapore several times at the end of the 19th century. Singapore was his home-port for five months in the period 1887–1888, while he served as first mate on the *Vidar*, a steamboat that plied the trading routes of West Borneo and Celebes (now Sulawesi). The word has it that he conceived here *Lord Jim*, one of his masterpieces. Conrad's impressions of Singapore appeared in several of his stories, most notably in "The End of the Tether". His contribution to making Singapore and Southeast Asia more known to the western world was recognised by Singapore's National Heritage Board. A commemorative plaque to his honour, officially unveiled by Polish President Aleksander Kwaśniewski, on his 2004 visit can now be found near the Fullerton Hotel.

Yet another Pole, Czesław Słania — a world-renowned stamp and currency note engraver — made several series of stamps for Singapore Post, including a 1999 stamp issue featuring the first President of Singapore, Mr. Yusof Ishak. A printing plate of the series which commemorates the president is one of the highlights of the Singapore Philatelic Museum collection. The image Czesław Słania engraved was not just used for stamps, but also for the currency notes that Singapore uses now.

However, the most important to mention is the story of Krystyn Olszewski who played a somewhat less known but considerable role in Singapore's development. He was a Polish urban and town planner who contributed to the current design of the Lion City in many ways. A professional with extensive international experience in regional, urban and transport planning, Olszewski came first to Singapore in 1968 at the invitation of Mr. Lee Kuan Yew. He was appointed Chief Designer of Singapore's Comprehensive Long-Term Concept Plan. The plan was officially announced in 1971 and most of its fundamental proposals have since been successfully implemented, leading to Singapore as we know it now. It envisaged the development of new townships in a ring formation around the central water catchment area, a network of expressways and a mass rapid transit (MRT) system, and a new international airport to be located at Changi. The main features of the plan can already be traced on the map drawn and signed by Olszewski in 1969. A *Straits Times* article from 9 April 1971 gives the account of his presentation of the concept plan. Subsequently, Olszewski was a planning consultant for several important projects. He originated the concept of Marina City and designed the Singapore Science Park at Kent Ridge. As a Senior Architect with the Mass Rapid Transit Corporation, he was also responsible for the architectural design and implementation of seven of the elevated MRT stations.

One of Singapore's planners and builders, Olszewski is one of those who should be particularly remembered on the occasion of Singapore's 50th anniversary. He was a Pole by birth but Singaporean at heart. He spent in Singapore a total of 15 active years of his professional career and contributed with his craft and expertise to building up Singapore in its initial years. A Pole among Singapore's pioneers, one may say. Perhaps, in recognition of his contributions, a street in the city centre that he helped to reshape or one of MRT stations that he designed could be named after him, even if his Polish surname seems difficult to pronounce. As for pronunciation, Olszewski himself came up with a simple method to help his Singaporean friends remember and pronounce his name: he would tell them, all you need to remember is just three English words and say it as if it was one word: "All-chefs-ski".

The story of Polish people in Singapore continues. Nowadays, Singapore is home to around 800 Polish people, most of them highly qualified professionals, in particular in the banking and IT sectors and businessmen. Singapore's growing position as one of the academic and scientific hubs of Asia is also a magnet for ambitious Polish students and achieved scientists. One of the most known Poles in Singapore is Professor Wiesław Nowiński who was Director of the Biomedical Imaging Lab of A*STAR until December 2014, and a creator of the most advanced human brain atlases. (Another article in this publication looks more specifically at his career and its contributions.) His team of researchers was the first to introduce brain atlases into clinical practice, allowing applications such as the treatment of stroke through computer-aided diagnosis and detection. A recipient of numerous scientific accolades, Professor Nowiński was named Pioneer in Medicine 2013 by the Society of Brain Mapping and Therapeutics in recognition of his significant scientific contribution in the area of brain mapping. He has also presented his work in the US Congress. He spent over 20 years of his scientific career in Singapore working on innovative research projects with his Singaporean colleagues. The recent Memorandum of Understanding in scientific cooperation between Poland and Singapore, signed in Warsaw during Prime Minister Lee's visit, creates prospects for more of ground-breaking cooperation of this kind.

A brief reflection on the aforementioned visit seems an appropriate way to conclude this contribution. Prime Minister Lee paid his first official visit to Poland in 2013 in the course of his sole trip to Europe that year (visiting Poland and France). He met with his Polish counterpart Donald Tusk (who is now the President of the European Council) and called on other Polish leaders. During the trip, Prime Minister Lee went to Warsaw but also, together with Prime Minister Tusk, to Gdańsk — the home city of Lech Wałęsa and the cradle of the Solidarity movement. During his visit Mr. Lee noted that Singapore's success is part of the reason that countries such as Poland are interested in engaging and doing business with Singapore but also recognised the success of the Polish transformation over the last 25 years. Speaking at the Bilateral Poland-Singapore Business Forum, he remarked that Poland is regarded as one of Europe's bright lights which Singapore is keen to engage with. It was, in fact, an expression of both countries' intentions when he said that just as Singapore can be a gateway for Polish companies in Asia, Poland can fulfil the same function for Singaporean companies looking to Europe, in particular central and Eastern Europe. Several recently concluded agreements, such as the bilateral double taxation treaty, the open skies agreement, as well as the important Singapore-EU FTA, are laying the grounds for a closer and more intense cooperation. Far and beyond any agreements, the kindred spirit of both Singaporean and Polish people in pursuing excellence and entrepreneurship should guarantee years of successful cooperation between our two countries to come.

. . . . .

The essay draws from an earlier article by H.E. Zenon Kosiniak-Kamysz which appeared in The Straits Times on 27 December 2014.

H.E. Zenon Kosiniak-Kamysz is Ambassador of Poland to Singapore, and Katarzyna Kryczka is Press Officer at the Embassy of Poland in Singapore.

Singapore and Slovakia — Friendly Countries with a Strong Story

Michal Slivovič

A glamorous city-state, a homeland of different nations, cultures and religions, a place well connected with the rest of the world, is celebrating its 50th birthday. Connectivity is a fashionable term in today's parlance and, at the same time, also an important message for Europe and Asia — an imperative for our joint economic prosperity and sustainable development. The following remarks aim to highlight the connection between my home country and the country to which I am accredited — Slovakia and Singapore.

At first glance it seems these two countries have nothing in common. The former is a landlocked country set in the very heart of Europe, a fully-fledged member of European and Euro Atlantic integration structures; the latter an island country located close to the Equator, geographically part of South East Asia.

However, when looking more deeply and attentively, one can find many similarities and a longstanding relationship between the two countries — proof that in today's world, geographical distance does not matter as long as there is a will to engage, cooperate and develop a serious partnership.

Singapore and Slovakia are relatively small countries and have almost the same population size of five and a half million people. We are not rich in terms of natural resources, but endowed in terms of human capital, and we enjoy a relatively young statehood (Singapore being a little bit older). Last but not least, we are even alphabetical neighbours in the international community, which enables us to be seated next to each other during international forums and meetings.

More importantly, both Slovakia and Singapore offer compelling stories of vision and gumption. Singapore was a rather undeveloped country at the outset of its independence in the 1960s, but had two strong assets. Skilled leaders offered far-reaching visions and resolve to make bold strategic decisions in regard to directing the country, while hardworking people were willing to accept and properly implement these visions. The outcome is there for everyone to see — Singapore has been turned into a financial and logistical hub with political and economic reach extending far beyond the region. At the same time, it also serves as an example of a well-functioning multi-ethnic society. The successful transformation of Singapore, which has catapulted the city-state to the top spots in various international rankings, thus offers many valuable lessons for smaller countries that lack significant natural resources and have to rely on their human capital.

After the peaceful dissolution of the former Czecho-Slovak Federation on 1 January 1993, many people spoke about how unsustainable the new, young state would prove to be. Certainly, the process of the building of our statehood was neither easy nor straightforward. There were some ups and downs on this path and painful reforms — immense both in scope and depth. However, at the end of the day we were able to realise our ambitions to be firmly anchored in the family of the most advanced European nations as a deeply integrated member state of the European Union, thus being an integral part of a peaceful, democratic, prosperous and stable community of nations.

Slovakia and Singapore are approximately in the same "weight category". We share the fate of smaller countries. We are destined to cooperate, having identical or very similar positions on many international issues, a common interest in building peace, security and stability in the world, and face comparable security challenges.

It fills me with joy to note that relations between Slovakia and Singapore have long been friendly and have successfully developed into a genuine partnership. A very good level of mutual political dialogue has been reflected in numerous visits at top political levels. Just to mention a few: former Slovak President Ivan Gašparovič paid an official visit to Singapore in 2006, and Singaporean Senior Minister Goh Chok Tong visited Slovakia in the same year. A reciprocal official visit of President Tony Tan followed in November 2013, symbolically in the year when we were celebrating the 20th anniversary of the establishment of bilateral diplomatic relations. The visit confirmed the quality of our ties and the mutual interest in their further deepening.

I would like to discuss briefly the latest bilateral activity, the visit of Miroslav Lajčák, Deputy Prime Minister and Minister of Foreign and European Affairs of Slovakia to Singapore, which took place in November 2014 — exactly one year after the visit of President Tan to Slovakia. The frequency of these encounters again proves the strength of the partnership between our countries.

The aim of Deputy Prime Minister Lajčák's visit was to build on the positive momentum in our bilateral relations and, in addition to continuing our excellent political dialogue, to explore concrete opportunities for cooperation in other fields such as trade, investment, science, research, innovation and technology. Slovakia stands ready to learn and apply lessons from Singapore´s transformation experience. This was also reflected in the composition of the Slovak delegation, which included the Minister of Justice, business representatives and the Chairman of the Slovak Academy of Sciences.

In the course of his intensive visit, Minister Lajčák met top Singaporean officials, namely President Tony Tan, Prime Minister Lee Hsien Loong, Minister for Foreign Affairs and for the Law K. Shanmugam, Minister for Environment and Water Resources Vivian Balakrishnan and Minister for Trade and Industry Lim Hng Kiang. Both sides exchanged views on a range of bilateral, regional and global issues and the visit further advanced our bilateral ties in a number of areas of common interest.

Minister Lajčák and Minister Lim officially launched the Singaporean-Slovak Business Forum in the premises of the Singapore Business Federation. It offered unique opportunities for the introduction of Slovakia as an attractive investment destination to potential Singaporean investors, a presentation of a dozen Slovak companies, and a chance to establish contacts between entrepreneurs and direct business and trade negotiations.

This gradual strengthening of contacts between our business people is an encouraging sign. Writing as a representative of the one of the European Union's member states, I would also like to express my strong belief that the early ratification of the PCA and FTA between the EU and Singapore would be a step in the right direction — putting mutual relations at a new level and boosting our bilateral economic ties.

Slovakia recognises numerous achievements of Singapore in the field of research, science, technology and innovations and the successful linkage between scientists, R&D institutions and business. In this regard, the talks of the Chairman of the Slovak Academy of Sciences at the Agency for Science, Technology and Research (A*STAR), Biomedical Research Council, National Medical Research Council, National University of Singapore and Nanyang Technological University focused on concrete joint research projects. We hope that at least some of them will be carried out in the foreseeable future.

As I have spoken about innovations, this is the right moment to mention one of the Slovak success stories in this field that has a direct connection with Singapore — the Slovak company ESET has grown into a global brand, becoming one of the global leaders in IT security. They have been protecting their customers' digital environment for more than 25 years. They have become one of the pioneers of cyber-security and have been expanding business activities in the Asia-Pacific region from their regional headquarters in Singapore.

Singapore is known in Slovakia for its highly favourable business environment and hardworking people, but also for stability, safety, high quality services, quality of life and sensitivity to the environment. Naturally, these benchmarks attract and lure people from all around the world, including my country. People-to-people contacts contribute to the increase of mutual awareness and thus represent an integral and inseparable part of relations between both countries. These are not just about politics or economy but also about people, about their everyday lives and emotions. Nowadays, more than a hundred Slovaks call Singapore their second home, contributing to the diversity and dynamics of Singaporean society. It goes without saying that their success is also the success of Slovakia and Singapore.

I must mention at least one of these success stories that bring our countries closer together. It is the remarkable story of a charming lady, whose life mission is to help people as gastroenterologist and hepatologist. Dr. Andrea Rajnakova, after attaining her medical degree in Slovakia, followed her husband in 1995 to Singapore, where she completed a Doctorate in Medical Studies (PhD) with a speciality in gastric cancer at the National University of Singapore. After the award of her degree she practised as a gastroenterologist and hepatologist at the National University Hospital until 2010. Dr. Rajnakova always showed passion in research and teaching and in passing on her knowledge and experience to junior doctors and medical students. She is well published in international journals and received several prestigious research and clinical awards. Currently she is practising at Mount Elizabeth Hospital in Singapore. In November 2014 she was presented the Goodwill Envoy award by Minister Lajčák for spreading the good name of Slovakia abroad.

In conclusion, 50 years is rather short time in global history, but it can mean a lot for a new country. It shows whether a country is a failing state or a success story. Singapore followed the latter path, proving that the past five decades have not been spent in vain. History teaches us that such a development cannot be taken for granted. I wholeheartedly wish Singapore further successful navigation of the vibrant waters of world affairs in the years to come. Singapore deserves it.

H.E. Michal Slivovič is Ambassador of Slovakia to Brunei, Indonesia, the Philippines, Singapore, Timor Leste and ASEAN. He is resident in Jakarta.

Section 3

From Commerce and Industry to Education and Science

From Central Europe to Singapore: Bata and Baťa

Tomáš Smetánka

Bata is a name Singaporeans have been familiar with for more than eight decades, since the first shoes imported from Czechoslovakia were offered in a *Yap Heng* store in 1926. As in many other countries worldwide, the name has become associated with footwear, while its Czech connection has been obscured or lost. The fascinating story of the first and so far the only Czech who created a truly global brand and a multinational company is one that bears witness to the inception of trade and investment ties between the Central-European country and Singapore.

Tomáš Baťa (although the peculiar Czech accent over *t* in the founder's surname was discernible in the company logo all the way until the 1940s, we will use it here when speaking of the person in a distinction from the firm) was a man who — in the words of a Straits Times reporter of 1931 — "was a village cobbler's son and in his time peddled boots and shoes from door to door", who became "an industrial peril to England and America and the boot and shoe king of the world."[1] By the time of the publication of the article, Mr. Baťa, at the age of 55, was commanding the world's greatest boot and shoe company with 17,000 employees, 2,000 retail shops, and output of 135,000 pairs of shoes a day.

One of those retail shops was located in Singapore, and it opened on 11 February 1931 in the Capitol Building on North Bridge Road. The newspaper ad of the store opening brought a message of a mass production that enables the company to sell shoes "at ridiculously low prices" and the slogan of "Quality higher than the Price".[2] If one takes newspaper ads at face value, the new Bata store must have been an immediate success: In less than a month from the opening, one could

---

[1] *The Straits Times*, 18 June 1931.
[2] *The Straits Times*, 10 February 1931.

read that "within a few weeks practically all stocks were sold out. Proof positive that never before has Singapore known such revolutionary prices for Shoes." The company then announced that it appreciated "the unfamiliar Sizes and Styles existing here and, therefore, the huge European factory has produced 'SPECIAL' sizes and styles" for the Singaporean branch.[3]

Regardless of how many shoes were sold in Singapore, the renown of Mr. Baťa as a great entrepreneur had reached the Crown Colony before he arrived in person in January 1932. He set out for the journey to the Middle East, India and Southeast Asia by one of his company's respectable fleet of planes and his travels were well followed by the press. The Batavia correspondent of The Straits Times brought the news of Baťa's departure from Europe on 17 December 1931, floating the idea of his visit to Singapore to be in connection with the establishment of a factory and the purchase of a rubber estate. "It has been the principle of the Bata firm to produce in the country in which it sells," the report stated.[4]

The advent of the Czech would-be investor raised no small expectations: representatives of several firms had been sent to Siam, Burma and India to meet him prior to his arrival to Singapore. Other companies dispatched cables to places Mr. Baťa was likely to visit with instructions that he be approached concerning possible supplies for his building of a factory in Singapore.[5]

However, when the "Shoe King" landed in Singapore on 19 January 1932, there were only two people at the Seletar Air Base to meet him, his company manager for Malaya and a reporter from The Straits Times. "At every place in the East I have been I have seen thousands of people walking about without shoes," said Mr. Baťa to the latter. "I have been told the reason is that they cannot afford to buy them. I am going to encourage the wearing of rubber shoes and manufacture and sell them at as low a price as possible." In the car on his way to the city, Baťa corrected the paper's previous reports: "I am here to buy rubber and sell shoes. Before I make any definite decision about a factory I must study the country and its condition." He then confirmed he intended to build a factory in India. "But Singapore? I have made no definite decision yet."[6]

A day later, having spent hours with local businessmen, Baťa commented favourably on the business conditions, saying Singapore was far more advanced than he had thought. He then acknowledged that he had begun to realise different shoes were needed in different climates and for different classes of workers. India on one hand and Malaya plus the Dutch East Indies on the other did not seem to

---
[3] *The Straits Times*, 5 March 1931.
[4] *The Straits Times*, 17 December 1931.
[5] *The Straits Times*, 17 January 1932.
[6] *The Straits Times*, 20 January 1932.

him as one market any more, implying the possibility of starting production in Southeast Asia.[7]

This was the time when British Malaya imported about 67,000 pairs of shoes in six months, of which 15,000 were from the UK, 4,500 from the US and 23,000 from continental Europe. The quantity grew by more than a quarter from the previous year "due in large measure to the activities of a large Czecho-Slovak firm which was establishing a chain of stores throughout the Far East," the American Trade Commissionaire in Singapore reported.[8]

Before Tomáš Baťa returned home from his Asian journey, newspapers informed readers about his intention to launch a scheduled air connection between Czechoslovakia and Southeast Asia to serve his business interests and for an air mail service.[9] Had this idea come true, Czechoslovakia would have been only the third European country — after the Netherlands and the UK — to enjoy regular commercial flights to Singapore.

It is hard to ascertain to what extent the tragic death of Tomáš Baťa on 12 July 1932 caused the audacious plan to remain unfulfilled. The great proponent and promoter of flying lost his life in a plane crash after taking off for a business trip within Europe, but the aviation sector of the company continued to thrive, together with the whole Bata enterprise, under the leadership of Jan A. Baťa, the founder's half-brother and successor.

Among other things, material and immaterial, Jan took over his relative's maxim "The air is our ocean" and followed his steps to Asia on a round-the-world business journey that brought him to Singapore, too. He registered at Raffles Hotel in February 1937 as a "shoemaker". No more rumours were published about a new factory by the time of Jan A. Baťa's visit; there was one newly operational in the city of Klang, Selangor, which opened in 1936. "The shoemaker", however, made headlines by his address at the Rotary Club on the danger that suppliers of rubber may face from the synthetic material produced in Germany and Russia for half of the current price of the natural stuff. He also mentioned that out of the 40 to 50 million pairs of shoes produced annually by Bata worldwide, about 300,000 were exported to Malaya.[10] This would mean the company's export increased six times within five years.

The year of "the shoemaker's" visit to Singapore and his return to the company's Czech headquarters via China, Hawaii and North America was to remain a period of the utmost success and freedom of the Bata global organisation for many years

---

[7] *Singapore Free Press and Mercantile Advertiser*, 21 January 1932.
[8] *Singapore Free Press and Mercantile Advertiser*, 21 January 1932.
[9] *The Straits Times*, 28 January 1932.
[10] *Singapore Free Press and Mercantile Advertiser*, 11 February 1937.

to come. Soon after, all development and decisions were to be forced in a direction moulded by the politics, economic losses, occupation and war.

When Czechoslovakia was obliged to cede its border regions to Germany by the Munich Agreement of 1938, equipment from Bata plants in those areas was hastily dismounted, removed and dispatched overseas, together with complete crews ready to start production in various countries. A set of machines sent away just before Hitler's forces completed the occupation of the country reached Singapore. The plans discussed and speculated about in 1932 finally materialised: The Bata factory was built and put into operation at the city's Prince Edward Road.

Journalists had been shown the new facility on the last day of January 1940. They saw "Chinese trained by Czecho-Slovak technicians at work on an endless belt unit comprising 35 machines and capable of producing at least 1,000 pairs of shoes a day. Work that takes an hour by hand is done in a few minutes by the machines, the most modern of their kind, observed a reporter, adding that the splendid factory organisation, which includes a special printing department, is a small replica of the system that has made the name of Bata world famous."[11] In the words of another reporter, "the system that made Zlin, the headquarters of Thomas Bata's shoe factory, the greatest shoe-manufacturing city in the world has been translated — with some modifications — to Singapore."[12]

Alas, it was not long before the war that thwarted Mr. Bata's plans in his home country reached Singapore. The Czech community of the Bata company joined the Straits Settlement Volunteer Force in their heroic defence against the Japanese onslaught, but the total destruction of the Crown Colony did not spare the Bata factory either.

Bata resumed business in Singapore just a couple of months after the war in January 1946 and developed sales, services and production in the country again. By that time, however, the Czech connection had been loosened as the company headquarters had moved to Canada. The following expropriation of all Bata assets in Czechoslovakia by the ascending revolutionary regime severed the ties between Bata Company and Bata family with their homeland for four long decades. They were decades of growth and development of Bata under the direction of Tomáš J. Bata, the founder's son, in many countries other than Czechoslovakia.

After the long separation, Mr. Bata Jr. finally came back to his father's hometown of Zlín in December 1989, to an enthusiastic and emotional welcome that became symbolic of the fall of the communist rule in Czechoslovakia. The network of Bata shops had been restored throughout the country soon after and the Bata company took over a shoe factory in Zlín Region, close to the place where it all

---

[11] *The Straits Times*, 1 February 1940.
[12] *Singapore Free Press and Mercantile Advertiser*, 1 February 1940.

had started one century earlier. The plant produces hand sewn shoes that are exported, among other destinations, to Singapore.

Bata of today is headquartered in Lausanne, Switzerland, and led by Thomas G. Bata, the grandson of the founder. The company serves one million customers each day, selling about 270 million pairs of shoes in more than 70 countries. Singapore is the seat of its Asia-Pacific business unit.

H.E. Tomáš Smetánka is the Ambassador of the Czech Republic to Indonesia, Brunei, Singapore and Timor Leste, resident in Jakarta.

From Palm Oil to Consumer Goods' Giant

Benjamin Felix van Roij

The Anglo-Dutch multinational company Unilever, well known worldwide for its consumer goods, was founded in 1929 when the British soap maker Lever Brothers merged with the Dutch margarine producer Margarine Unie. The merger of the two companies made commercial sense because they both used the raw material palm oil for the production of margarines and soap. In the second half of the 20th century Unilever diversified and expanded its business globally.

In the year 2014 Unilever celebrated its 85th anniversary and is one of the oldest multinational companies in the world. Their portfolio includes processed food, beverages, household cleaning agents and a variety of personal care and hygiene products. Its products are being sold in around 190 countries and on any given day almost two billion people use Unilever products. In that sense their lives are being touched by the enterprise in many different ways. So the company's corporate vision is quite tangibly true: "Helping people to look good, feel good and get more out of life."

The enterprise consists of two companies: Unilever NV based in Rotterdam and Unilever PLC based in London. Both locations operate as singular business units but with a common board of directors. Together with America's Procter & Gamble and Switzerland's Nestlé, Unilever is one of the world's largest consumer goods companies with more than 174,000 employees, more than 400 different brands, a total turnover of almost €50 billion and a net profit of €5.3 billion (2013).

For Unilever, sustainability is an integral part of its business strategy and sustainable growth is the only acceptable model of growth for the multinational. In line with this ambitious strategy, Unilever has launched Project Sunlight, a project which tries to move people to create a more sustainable way of life. Unilever's initiative encourages them to join what Unilever sees as "a growing community of people who want to make the world a better place for children and future generations." Unilever believes that it has a responsibility not only to their consumers but also to the communities and the regions in which the company has a presence. That is why Unilever invests in local economies and tries to develop people's skills inside and outside of the company.

Innovation is also a key factor for a company like Unilever to enhance its brands and improve the products' taste, fragrance or functionality. Unilever annually invests almost €1 billion in research and development. At Unilever there are over 6,000 R&D professionals who work in the six global research centres, 13 global product development centres and regional and country development and implementation centres. Unilever believes that success is only possible when acting with "the highest standards of corporate behaviour towards our employees, consumers and the societies and world in which we live," and Project Sunlight is a great example of how big influential companies can contribute to the world we live in and make sustainability a commonplace.

Unilever in Singapore

The business of Unilever in Singapore was established more than 60 years ago (in 1954). It started as a trading agency (Lever Brothers Malaya) for its detergent and edible fats business. Today Unilever Singapore has become a strategic global hub and the office here houses important members of Unilever's senior leadership team. The global functions which the Singapore office undertakes are, among others, brand development, supply chain management, customer development and finance. The company also manufactures some of Unilever's most important and globally sold products. It is the regional business headquarters for ASEAN and the Australasia region. Unilever's Food Solutions is also based in Singapore. At this moment the Singapore office is one of six departments globally to house Unilever's Customer Insight and Innovation Centre for shoppers' behaviour.

According to Mr. Hein Swinkels, former CFO of subsidiary Unilever Nederland B.V. (2002–2006) and Vice President of Finance Unilever Thailand (2006–2012), Lever Brothers entered Malaysia (Malaya) in connection with the sourcing of palm oil. "This happened somewhere at the end of the 19th century. Later on Marketing Sales operations were established in Singapore and the rest of the region to supply Sunlight Soap and other products to the local consumers." Some 35 years ago, he adds, operations were streamlined around the Singapore hub: "Singapore became the regional head office in the 1980s, while in 2005 all key marketing and supply chain functions were moved from the various local Unilever Operating Companies in the region to Singapore, to establish a more harmonised and efficient business by leveraging brands and scale." Currently the complete Asian Supply Chain is centrally managed from the Singapore office. "Attractive incentives offered by the EDB [Singapore Economic Development Board], such as tax holidays et cetera, was an important factor in the choice for Singapore as the strategic global hub," Mr. Swinkels continues.

In June 2013 Unilever opened and established a €50 million research and training department called "Four Acres", located in the heart of Singapore's international research and development hub Biopolis, and this centre will train and educate a larger group of talented future leaders who will help Unilever sustain its consistent growth over the past few years. The department will develop new professionals from all over the world based on Unilever's "purpose-driven" approach for doing business. Mr. Swinkels explains that this establishment is "based on the famous Four Acres in Kingston upon Thames, England", a state-of-the-art training facility which has set the standard in leadership development for the past 60 years. "This centre aims to develop and train new (Asian) executives. Developing key talent and leadership is crucial for the sustained success of any business. Unilever has been particularly strong in this respect and always invest in its people, as they are the company's most important 'assets'." The company's choice to locate the new leadership development facility in Singapore highlights Unilever's rising focus on the emerging markets across the world, especially ASEAN, which already account for more than 55% of the worldwide revenue and according to Unilever Singapore is the logical choice for the new campus. The company plays a significant role in the market and Singapore is already the enterprise's global operations hub. The aim for the Singaporean based training facility is to provide more than 50% of all of Unilever's worldwide leadership development programmes.

Since Singapore's independence in 1965, the country has grown enormously on the economic level. This rapid growth is one of the key reasons for locating Unilever's regional head office here. "Of course Singapore became more and more attractive as a regional head office. There was a lot of local talent, very good infrastructure and decent expat conditions for European Unilever employees," Mr. Swinkels explains. Today Singapore is a very important link between the developed and the emerging economies: It is a leading hub for innovation and leadership and geographically is the gateway for the fast emerging ASEAN economies. Business relations with Europe are still strong. "Unilever sources many raw materials from all over the globe," Mr. Swinkels continues, "for example palm oil from Indonesia and Malaysia to be used in the margarine production back in Europe." In response to the deforestation and other environmental concerns, Unilever has made a commitment to sustainably source all their palm oil by the year 2015. In 2013 the company even launched a special policy (Unilever's Sustainable Palm Oil Sourcing Policy) to stop deforestation, protect peat lands and bring positive impact to local communities. "All the procurement is done by a global team which is based in

Rotterdam. This team will get, whenever necessary, regional support from their colleagues based in Singapore," Mr Swinkels adds. The Singapore office mainly focuses on ASEAN countries but also services the greater Asia-Pacific. Nonetheless the relationship with Europe and the European Union could always be strengthened. According to Mr. Swinkels, "Unilever could do more in that sense, for example by increasing exchange and cooperation in the field of innovation, in building more far-reaching and modern technology centres and help with training and educational methods."

Singapore and the Asian region are still growing rapidly. For consumer companies like Unilever that brings great opportunities. Because of the location, Singapore creates an ideal base for doing business in the rest of the region. Singapore provides a wide range of professional services to help establish Unilever's activities. According to Unilever's CEO Paul Polman, Singapore has "superb business infrastructure, excellent human capital, connectivity and strong base of supporting industries combined with the support provided by the Singapore Government make it an ideal place for a regional business hub." The company's investments in Singapore reflect the future oriented commitment to Singapore and the ambitions for the rest of the region. "The future of Unilever in Singapore and the region is very interesting. The living conditions are good in Singapore and hopefully this remains that way," Mr. Swinkels explains. "From a business perspective there should always be a correct balance between local hired employees and expats. On a personal level I find Singapore well organised, but a bit too plastic for me. There is not enough space and people are very money oriented. Happiness is of course more than money and the locals seem very unhappy."

Building on the old Unilever heritage "feel good, look good and get more out of life", today's priorities are more and more influenced by Unilever's sustainable living strategy. The company's strong sense of corporate social responsibility should move not only other companies to do the same, but also engender strong permanent responsibilities for making the world more sustainable for the next generations. Perhaps here lies an important opportunity for the new Singapore-trained leaders.

References

DutchCham Singapore, (n.d.). Unilever to Set Up Global Leadership Centre in S'pore. Retrieved 3 March 2015 from http://fourteen-and-nine.net/olddutchcham/unilever-to-set-up-global-leadership-centre-in-spore.

Economic Development Board (EDB). (2014). Unilever: Driving Business and Talent Strategies Across Asia and the World. Retrieved 3 March 2015 from https://www.edb.gov.sg/content/edb/en/case-studies/unilever.html.

Interview, November, 2014, with Mr. Hein Swinkels, former CFO Unilever B.V. Nederland and former Vice President of Finance Unilever Thailand.

MarketWatch. (2014, January 10). Unilever Announces Final Results 2013. Retrieved 3 March 2015 from http:// www.marketwatch.com/story/unilever-announces-final-results-2013-2014-01-21.

Project Sunlight (n.d.). What is Project Sunlight? Retrieved 3 March 2015 from https://www.projectsunlight.com.

Unilever. (2013, November 20). Unilever launches Project Sunlight — A New Initiative to Inspire Sustainable Living. Retrieved 3 March 2015 from http://www.unilever.com/mediacentre/pressreleases/2013/Unileverlaunchesprojectsunlightanewinitiativetoinspiresustainableliving.aspx.

Unilever. (2014a). Introduction to Unilever. Retrieved 3 March 2015 from http://www.unilever.com/aboutus/introductiontounilever.

Unilever. (2014b). Our History. Retrieved 3 March 2015 from http://www.unilever.com/aboutus/ourhistory/.

Unilever. (2014c). Unilever at a Glance. Retrieved 3 March 2015 from http://www.unilever.com/aboutus/introductiontounilever/unileverataglance/.

Unilever. (2015). Palm Oil Infographic. Retrieved 3 March 2015 from http://www.unilever.com/sustainable-living-2014/reducing-environmental-impact/sustainable-sourcing/sustainable-palm-oil/Palmoilinfographic/index.aspx.

Unilever Singapore. (2013, June 28). Unilever Opens €50m Leadership Development Facility. Retrieved 3 March 2015 from http://www.unilever.com.sg/aboutus/newsandmedia/pressreleases/Unilever_Opens_Euro50m_Leadership_Development_Facility.aspx.

Unilever Singapore. (2014a). Introduction to Unilever. Retrieved 3 March 2015 from http://www.unilever.com.sg/aboutus/introductiontounilever/.

Unilever Singapore. (2014b). Our History. Retrieved 3 March 2015 from http://www.unilever.com.sg/aboutus/ourhistory/.

Benjamin Felix van Roij is a Master student at KU Leuven. He was an Associate at the EU Centre from September to December 2014.

Jebsen & Jessen (SEA) — A Singapore Story with European Roots

Benjamin Felix van Roij

Jebsen & Jessen (SEA), with its headquarters in Singapore, is a diversified engineering, manufacturing and distribution group that has worked since 1963 "in partnerships with global market leaders, facilitating and capitalising on opportunities throughout South East Asia". The Singaporean company is part of a global family enterprise which started as a trading partnership formed in Hong Kong at the end of the 19th century. Jebsen & Jessen (SEA) has just celebrated its 50th anniversary with the slogan "Together for Tomorrow".

Jebsen & Jessen (SEA) is one of Singapore's most successful family-owned businesses, operating in nine out of the ten ASEAN member countries. The company has eight regional business units, all with leading positions in their particular markets. 2013 turnover was S$1.2 billion, with a headcount of 4,300 people and over 20,000 customers.

What are the origins of Jebsen & Jessen (SEA)?

In March 1895 Jacob Jebsen and Heinrich Jessen left their hometown Aabenraa, in what was then the Duchy of Schleswig (today part of the Kingdom of Denmark and part of the *Euroregion* Sønderjylland-Schleswig). They established their company Jebsen & Co in Hong Kong. Both Jebsen and Jessen came from seafaring families. They started out as agents of the M. Jebsen (Jacob Jebsen's father) shipping company. As the company grew, they established new offices in Shanghai and Guangzhou. In 1909 they established Jebsen & Jessen in Hamburg. This company would coordinate the trading business and maintain the relationships between the firm in Asia and their European principals.

In the 1930s and 1940s the second generation of leaders, Heinz Jessen, Michael Jebsen, Hans Jacob Jebsen and Arwed Peter (known as AP) Jessen emerged and, by the 1950s, the company was expanding and diversifying. During the 1960s the new political environment in China raised questions regarding Jebsen & Co.'s future in Hong Kong as a business epicentre. One of these second generation partners in Jebsen & Co, A. P. Jessen, looked at the changes taking place in Asia, and saw possibilities in doing business with the emerging countries in Southeast Asia.

A. P. Jessen established the independent company Jebsen & Jessen in December 1963, with offices in Singapore and Kuala Lumpur, at the time both part of Malaysia. Today, almost 120 years after the Jebsen & Jessen Family Enterprise was founded, it is still run by family members on the basis of the same enduring principles which drove Jacob Jessen and Heinrich Jessen to start their business at the end of the 19th century. The enterprise continues to build sustainable business and remain entrepreneurial in spirit.

Third generation and present Chairman of Jebsen & Jessen (SEA), Heinrich Jessen, 47 years old and a trained biologist, highlights these family values during the interview and shows that today's link with Europe is based on a strong business relationship in that the company sources many of its products and components from Europe. He adds that "Jebsen & Jessen (SEA) acts in a number of our activities as distributors of European products." But next to this business relationship with Europe the company also has strong relational (family) roots with Europe.

Born a Dane, Heinrich Jessen is today a Singapore citizen. He explains that he and his family are "proud of our Southern Danish roots", but adds that "Jebsen & Jessen (SEA) is not a Danish enterprise." Jebsen & Jessen (SEA) has no office in Denmark or anywhere else in Europe. "We view ourselves as an ASEAN group; headquartered in Singapore, Singapore-owned but with strong European roots."

Today's Jebsen and Jessen Family Enterprise comprises five groups with a shared history, values system and ownership. The original company Jebsen & Co. still grows business across China, out of its Hong Kong headquarters; Jebsen & Jessen (SEA) operates across ASEAN; and in Hamburg Jebsen & Jessen distributes a range of goods across Europe. GMA headquartered in Perth, Australia, is the world's largest miner, processor and distributor of abrasive garnet; and Triton Textile sources garments in various Asian countries for export to Europe. The relationship between the three companies is "that of a big extended family but with each group working very much independently as an autonomous unit".

The icon of the family enterprise is the three mackerels, another connection with the European roots. The logo is an adaptation of the coat of arms of the founders' hometown of Aabenraa, Denmark. Heinrich Jessen explains: "The town of Aabenraa used the three mackerels' sign some 800 years ago. Located in a border region, the direction of the middle fish was changed whenever the town switched from being Danish to German and vice versa. When our company was founded in 1895, Aabenraa happened to be German and the middle fish was swimming in the opposite direction. Today Aabenraa is Danish and all three fish swim in the same direction."

After the booming period of the late 19th century and the beginning of the 20th century Jebsen & Co was severely hit by the First World War because it was considered to be a German company. One of the partners was even interned in Australia. After rebuilding in the 1920s, they lost almost everything again in the Second World War. Because of the events in China in the 1950s and 1960s following the Communist takeover, the 2nd generation was thinking whether they should have all their eggs in the Chinese basket. Hence, in 1963 one of the partners and father of current Chairman Heinrich Jessen, Arwed Peter (A. P.), decided to set up offices in Singapore and Kuala Lumpur simultaneously. "During that time there was already a lot of business in the region and Singapore had many characteristics like Hong Kong, an environment my father knew intimately," Jessen explains. "It was a natural choice."

After all these years the group's headquarters are still in Singapore although today Jebsen & Jessen (SEA) has eight business units, two of which have their HQs in Malaysia and two in Thailand. According to Heinrich Jessen, for operational headquarters Bangkok and Kuala Lumpur are just as good as Singapore but in terms of the holding company, Singapore is still the best. "There are tax benefits, there is the infrastructure, there is the reliability of the law, and there is the clean government. All these things make Singapore a very desirable place" to have the group headquarters.

Since 1993, with the creation of the single European market, Europe has become more open to competition. The single market also helped to create many new jobs, brought better prices for consumers and enabled both citizens and companies to benefit from a wider choice of goods and services. The Association of Southeast Asian Nations (ASEAN) similarly has the aspiration to create an ASEAN Economic Community by the end of 2015. Heinrich Jessen said, "I think the EU is to some degree a reference point for ASEAN with a few relevant benchmarks. But I do not think it is something ASEAN should want to copy or strive to emulate. The cultures in Europe are more similar to one another than the ones in the ASEAN countries."

Despite the grand plans of the AEC it has actually surprisingly little influence on the strategic thinking and business decisions of Jebsen & Jessen (SEA). This is probably a reflection of the fact that there is still much scepticism with regards to how integrated the AEC will be. "We are not making any strategic decisions based on AEC, whether AEC is achieved in 2015 or later, it will not change the kind of investments or decisions we are currently making."

Operating in the whole of ASEAN, Jebsen & Jessen (SEA) can claim to understand each of the ASEAN countries well. The knowledge of each of these countries is part of the value proposition they bring to their technology partners. Heinrich Jessen explains, "For our partners we make ASEAN look as if it is one country because we provide a uniform and integrated platform across the region. So the fact that ASEAN is actually so fragmented in a way is a business case for us. Clearly if ASEAN one day is truly integrated, it will also benefit us. In the long-term an integrated ASEAN is a very good thing for the region."

Over the past decades, Singapore and the Southeast Asian region have grown rapidly. A big part of Singapore's recent development is due to the Marina Area, and Jebsen & Jessen (SEA) has been part of this development. Many of its products can be found in the Marina Bay district, including a steam turbine and buggies in the Gardens by the Bay area, gondolas that go up and down most of the high-rise buildings to clean them and VOIP telephony systems that connect them, as well as the screw-jack based lifting system of the Event Plaza and foam-based geo-landscaping at both Marina Bay Sands and Gardens by the Bay. "You can say Marina Bay was a big part of Singapore's recent growth and we have our fingerprints on that," Jessen explains.

When Jebsen & Jessen (SEA) started in Singapore, they were basically acting as a middle man, sourcing for products in the European market and selling them in Southeast Asia. When there was a demand, the company brought in those products from Europe and supplied them to the customers here. But over time the Group started to value-add by designing, manufacturing and engineering their own products. They are even going to the next step where they are building and designing products here which they then sell back to Europe and elsewhere. "And that is I think very much a Singapore story as well," Jessen continues. "Singapore has a tradition of being eager to learn, looking throughout the world for good ideas and solutions, studying them intensely, and then applying them and building and improving on them forthwith."

Having been active in Singapore, Malaysia, Thailand and Indonesia since the 1960s and 1970s, Jebsen & Jessen (SEA) continued expanding in the region — adding the Philippines and Vietnam in the early 1990s and more recently Cambodia and Myanmar. The primary thrust of the Group's growth in the future will be technology transfer. "We want to move more aggressively up the value chain of designing our own products, building our own brands and in certain cases also moving beyond ASEAN whenever it makes sense, when there are global opportunities for some of the products that we make. So we will see more engineering, more manufacturing, more value-adding and maybe less emphasis on pure distribution," Jessen explains.

Ownership of the family enterprise is today concentrated with three members of the third generation — Heinrich Jessen, his brother, Peter Jessen and their cousin, Hans Michael Jebsen. One of the key challenges for a family business is always transition to the next generation and the question whether there are suitable and interested candidates who are capable to take the business to the next level. Jessen's own children are still young but within the two families the pool of possible future shareholders is of course growing. Next to that Jessen indicates that you could always go through a generation of non-family members running the enterprise. Asked whether the group has ever considered going public, Jessen maintains that, "We have no compelling reason to go public. You either go public because you need funds, and so far we have been able to finance our own growth, or because the owning family wishes to exit, which has never been the case."

As mentioned above, Jessen has given up his Danish passport and become a Singapore citizen. He has lived in many different countries all over the world but has decided to call Singapore home. "Singapore is in one sense like Australia, like America, a land where people came from all over the world and where many families have only lived for relatively few generations. Singapore is welcoming of new immigrants and this makes it very easy to decide to become a Singaporean citizen." At the same time Jessen is also proud of his European roots. "Our roots will always remain Danish and German. But I feel very proud of Singapore and what it has accomplished, and what it continues to accomplish, and the leadership it has shown to the world. It is a very pragmatic, it is a very forward-looking and it is a very intelligent country, and that makes it very easy to identify with."

References

Interview, on October 23, 2014, with Mr. Heinrich Jessen, Chairman of the Executive Board Jebsen & Jessen SEA.
Jebsen & Jessen (SEA). (2013). *50th Anniversary Brochure*.
Jebsen & Jessen (SEA). (2011a). *About Us*. Retrieved 3 March 2015 from http://www.jjsea.com/doc/AboutUs.
Jebsen & Jessen (SEA), (2011b). *Our History*. Retrieved 3 March 2015 from http://www.jjsea.com/doc/OurHistory.
Miller, L., and Wasmuth, A.C. (2008). *Three Mackerels: The Story of the Jebsen and Jessen Family Enterprise*. Hong Kong: Hongkongnow.com Ltd.
Nandin, Ines. (2014). Singapore: Knowledge and Network — Making Waves in the Offshore Industry. *Oil & Gas Financial Journal, 11*(10). Retrieved 3 March 2015 from http://www.ogfj.com/articles/print/volume-11/issue-10/features/focus-report-singapore/singapore-knowledge-and-network.html.

Benjamin Felix van Roij is a Master student at KU Leuven. He was an Associate at the EU Centre from September to December 2014.

Siemens in Singapore — Building Partnerships

Contribution from Siemens and Excel Marco

In 1847, Werner von Siemens and his business partner Johann Georg Halske started the Telegraphen-Bauanstalt von Siemens & Halske (Telegraph Construction Company of Siemens and Halske). This 10 men company formed the humble beginnings of what is now known as Siemens, Europe's largest engineering company and one of the world's biggest technology companies.

The company's early success was largely due to von Siemens' invention of the pointer telegraph. By electrically synchronizing the transmitter and receiver, the company was able to make an apparatus which had a range of 50 km, far superior at that time to any of its competitors.

In the following years, the company went on to make a name for itself by achieving success in areas such as building the first European long-distance telegraph line between Berlin and Frankfurt am Main in 1848 before becoming a publically held company in 1897.

Today, almost 170 years later, Siemens is a global conglomerate with factories and offices in more than 200 regions and around 343,000 employees worldwide. Siemens offers a wide range of solutions across industries ranging from healthcare to energy. In 2014, the company generated revenue of approximately €71.9 billion with a net income of €5.5 billion.

Siemens in Singapore — Growing Together

In 1908, Siemens established a technical office in Singapore to provide sales support for London-based Siemens Brothers Dynamo Works Ltd. and to source for new business opportunities in the flourishing British colony. The company realised that Singapore had the geographic advantage and potential to become a trade hub for the region.

A firm believer in partnerships, Siemens soon started building strong relations with several local companies and government agencies, demonstrating its commitment to Singapore and to the rest of the region.

Working with the local government, Siemens has helped to shape Singapore's infrastructure through various partnerships such as installing a highly efficient traction power supply for the country's new driverless metro line — the "Downtown Line" — with the Land Transport Authority (LTA). The company has also set up the Clinical Imaging Research Centre (CIRC) — a world-class R&D imaging facility to promote pioneering biomedical imaging research — with the Agency for Science, Technology and Research (A*Star).

Besides working with the Singapore government, Siemens has established partnerships with local small and medium enterprises (SMEs) in the region, providing them with free training and technical expertise to help them grow their business.

According to Mr. Raimund Klein, Executive Vice President and Head of Digital Factory (DF) and Process Industries & Drives (PD) divisions, Siemens ASEAN, "You need to build strong relationships and partnerships with local leaders and markets. One way to do so is to join hands with smaller companies, like local family businesses. Doing so will help you to better understand the local culture and business landscape."

Mr. Klein believes that these partnerships are mutually beneficial as they have helped Siemens to better understand the business climate and how Asian companies function. To date, Siemens DF and PD divisions have over 35 partnerships in Singapore and approximately 480 partners throughout Southeast Asia.

"Southeast Asia is an emerging market for Siemens and our focus here is value-added engineering. That is why we work with several contracted partners who are trained in our technology," Mr. Klein highlights.

The partnerships have allowed Siemens to grow together with Singapore, giving the company the opportunity to play an active part in Singapore's development into the regional economic stronghold and business hub that it is today.

Excel Marco

One of the contracted partners in Singapore is Excel Marco, a local onshore and offshore oil and gas, marine and logistics company. Established in 2000, the company has grown to a size of 100 employees and offers a wide range of technical services ranging from safety assessment and systems designs to turn-key systems integration of process controls.

Over 80 % of the company's operations currently involve providing automation solutions for offshore oil and gas exploration, drilling and production. These solutions are engineered to centrally control processes, acting like a brain for fixed platforms or Floating Production, Storage and Offloading (FPSOs). The platforms and FPSOs are designed to *extract* crude oil, *process*, pipe or *store* the oil until it can be off-loaded by shuttle tankers.

Excel Marco's unique and field-proven solutions help to "orchestrate" the harmonious integration of the critical processes equipment, and to ensure that the entire oil and gas production is optimised, and above all, safe.

Excel Marco also provides process safety solutions to its clients. These safety instrumented systems are primarily automatic safety controls designed to shut down the process during abnormal situations, protecting the people working on platforms or vessels, and making sure the assets remain intact by preventing any catastrophic events. In addition, the solutions help to protect the environment against pollution due to any inadvertent release of gas or oil leaks.

Siemens and Excel Marco — A Quality Partnership

Excel Marco is committed to providing their customers with the best German engineered solutions. Their focus on quality led them to source the majority of their components and solutions — over 70% — from Siemens.

Excel Marco's CEO and Managing Director Mr. David Ong said, "Siemens has a strong reputation for providing high quality and reliable engineering solutions. We became an official partner of Siemens since the inception of our business because of the perfect fit in our business philosophy and offering."

As part of the partnership, Siemens is committed to providing full knowledge transfer in process automation. This allows Excel Marco staff to improve their product knowledge and keep up-to-date with the latest Siemens innovations. This continuous training helped Excel Marco to grow its business and expertise over the years.

In 2008, Excel Marco became the first and only company outside Germany to be certified as a Solution Partner for Process Control System 7 (PCS7) and Process Safety Specialist. Today, Excel Marco is a well-known PCS7 system integrator, and a renowned Singaporean company on the world map, winning major projects around the globe.

The partnership with Siemens has not only helped Excel Marco grow in terms of its technical expertise, but it has also helped the company grow its customer base. Since 2011, Excel Marco has been the top provider for Siemens Process Automation Solutions. This led to Excel Marco being awarded the Siemens ASEAN Partner Excellence Award in 2012, 2013 and 2014.

"As a Siemens Solutions Partner, we have benefitted from the intensive training on their German technology which ensures that we provide quality solutions for customers," said Mr. Ong. "It has also opened up a greater customer base for our offerings."

Looking to the Future

The Siemens brand is built on the goal of achieving the highest performance with the highest ethics. The company strives to do business in a sustainable way by acting in the best interest of future generations — with respect to the economy, the environment and society. This extends to all aspects of its business from its operational processes to its corporate citizenship initiatives.

Siemens is continuously looking to provide long-term benefits in Singapore and the region and they hope to continue to be a part of Singapore's growth and success in the generations to come.

"Having been in Singapore for over 100 years, we have had the pleasure of growing with the country from a thriving port city under colonial rule, to its independence 50 years ago, and finally to the major trade and economic metropolis that it is today," said Mr. Klein. "We see a great future for Singapore and look forward to being a part of its future successes in the generations to come through maintaining our strong partnerships with the government and local companies such as Excel Marco."

References

Interview, on December 18, 2014, with Mr. David Ong, CEO and Managing Director of Excel Marco.

Interview, on December 19, 2014, with Mr. Raimund Klein, Executive Vice President and Head of Industry Siemens ASEAN.

Leong Ching (ed.). (2008). *Setting the Pace: Singapore 1908–2008* (Singapore: Siemens Pte. Ltd).

Siemens. (n.d.). *160 Years of Siemens. A Special Edition of SiemensWorld Celebrating the Company's Anniversary in October 2007*. Retrieved 3 March 2015 from http://www.siemens.com/history/pool/en/history/1847-1865_beginnings_and_initial_expansion/160j_e.pdf.

Siemens. (2012). Siemens Singapore. http://www.siemens.com/about/en/history.htm.

Siemens. (2014). At a Glance: Fiscal 2014. Retrieved 3 March 2015 from http://www.siemens.com/annual/14/en/download/pdf/Siemens_AR2014_At-a-glance.pdf.

Siemens. (2015). About Siemens. Retrieved 3 March 2015 http://www.siemens.com/about/en/.

Siemens. (2015). Sustainability at Siemens. Retrieved 3 March 2015 from http://www.siemens.com/annual/14/en/download/pdf/Siemens_AR2014_At-a-glance.pdf.

Siemens. (2015). The History of Siemens — From Workshop to Global Player. Retrieved 3 March 2015 from http://www.siemens.com/about/en/history.htm.

Science and Research Collaboration between Singapore and Europe

Bertil Andersson and Tony Mayer

The past 50 years have seen great changes in the world, not least in science and research, with incredible and rapidly moving advances, new disciplines arising and, of course, a total revolution in information and communications. During this time, we have also seen the development of new centres of intellectual endeavour. Fifty years ago, at the time of its independence, Singapore had to address many immediate challenges but through far-sighted investment in education at all levels and in research, the country has emerged at the forefront of research in the world and a key partner for Europe based on mutual academic esteem. During this same period, researchers, who have always exchanged ideas through the "Republic of Letters" have learned not only to exchange views and opinions but have learned how to really collaborate together in conducting their research and in sharing data and experiences, a procedure which has now become the global norm.

Of course some major collaborations predate the founding of the Republic of Singapore in 1965. For example, CERN *[the Conseil Européen pour la Recherche Nucléaire]*, the European Organization for Nuclear Research, was founded in 1954 and brought together high energy physicists based around a major research infrastructure — the Synchrocyclotron, built in 1975. Another example is the establishment of the European Molecular Biology Organisation (EMBO) which is now one year older than Singapore. In 1964, a group of leading life scientists came together to create an organisation to enable experimentalists of the then new discipline of molecular biology both to exchange ideas and to cooperate in creating a new laboratory. So in these early days, collaboration tended to be driven by the need to share the costs of creating major new infrastructures which their institutions or even their nations could not afford to do alone or to consolidate a new discipline.

Now we are in a new era of rapid expansion of research and its globalisation in which there is mobility not only of ideas but of people and institutions. Since the turn of the century, and despite the financial crisis of 2008/2009, the amount of global research investment has almost doubled with the number of researchers also having increased commensurately. In 2011, the Royal Society of London published "Knowledge, Networks and Nations" a report on global scientific collaboration. It found that accompanying this expansion of global research there has been another trend in which around 75% of all scientific papers are not only multi-authored but have authors coming from more than one institution. At the same time, the number of such collaborations, which involve international collaboration, now amounts to more than one third of all publications. Networking itself has become the norm and yet as late as the early 1970s, a scientific network in Europe organised through the COST (European Cooperation in Science and Technology) inter-Ministerial system was a mini-Treaty that required ratification by the national parliaments of the countries of those participating. Such cumbersome bureaucracy meant that networks were few and far between.

We are also seeing both an increase in the mobility of researchers and new patterns of mobility, especially of younger researchers, with a new "brain flow" pattern emerging. In place of the traditional trans-Atlantic brain flow between the US and Europe, there is now a triangular flow between Asia, Europe and the US which is a measure of how Asia is now recognised as an active contributor to global academic life, not the least being that of Singapore, an exemplar for others to follow. But this "brain flow" is not the only mobility as there is now a "mobility" of institutions with the establishment of branch campuses around the World. In our region, Malaysia has been active in encouraging branch campuses especially from UK universities (e.g. the Universities of Newcastle, Nottingham and Wales). In Singapore, there have been many examples of academic "inward investment" several of which have involved European universities. In addition to such developments, there has been the attraction of institutions on a comprehensive thematic research programme basis as is the case with the initiative by the Singapore National Research Foundation (NRF) — the Campus for Research Excellence and Technological Enterprise (CREATE) — which attracts top universities to Singapore to work on advanced research topics in partnership with local universities.

Since the early days after the Second World War, and especially over the past quarter of a century, several things have happened which have created the conditions for this new collaboration. We have seen the spread of high level research through a new level of commitment and development from Governments, especially within Asia and most especially within Singapore. Brains follow funding and this has meant that Singapore has become a player in the new "Champions

League" of research countries and very much the "new kid on the block". This is based on the impressive advances of, in particular, the Agency for Science, Technology and Research (A*STAR) and the two research-intensive universities, the National University of Singapore (NUS) and the Nanyang Technological University (NTU). The last named, NTU was only established as an independent body with its own charter in 1991, since when its rise into the top 40 universities in the World (QS World University Rankings 2014) has been exceptionally rapid, most of this occurring over the past half-decade or so. The level of development of research in Singapore has been impressive not just by its magnitude but especially by its rapidity with the country starting from a low base and now being on track to join an elite group of what we have called the "small, smart countries". These are the countries which have a very high rate of research investment measured by the percentage of GDP devoted to research and development — the Gross domestic expenditure on R&D (GERD) measure. These countries (Denmark, Finland, Israel, Sweden and Switzerland, now joined by Singapore) all have a GERD of around 3.0%. In Singapore's case, this target has been difficult to achieve, not because of the lack of investment but because of the very strong growth in overall GDP!

Under the current national strategy, Singapore is now investing a figure some 800% higher than at the start of 1991 when the country was only half its age (see Figure 1 below).

Singapore has always seen itself as a bridge between East and West and between North and South and so it is hardly surprising that its research collaborations have reflected these links. Historically, given the long colonial history of Singapore, it is to be expected that the bilateral relations between it and the UK are very strong. In this case, there has been a continuous and strong relationship with the UK which was highlighted by the State Visit of President Tony Tan to the UK in October 2014. Many of Singapore's leading personalities have been educated in

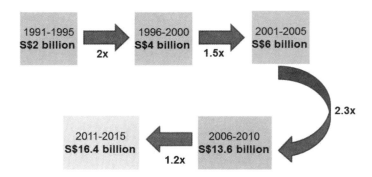

Figure 1. The increase in research funding as represented by the succession of five-year national R&D plans (Source: A*STAR).

the UK and research links are very strong. Perhaps one of the most exciting partnerships of recent years has been that between NTU and Imperial College London to create a new Medical School — the Lee Kong Chian School of Medicine — with cutting-edge teaching and attracting some of the leading medical brains to Singapore not only to teach but to lead forefront research teams. Apart from academic links, NTU has established strong partnerships with UK-based high technology multinational companies including Rolls-Royce.

There is, of course, the common "pull" of sharing a common language — English — and this has also meant that increasingly Singapore, with its increasingly global outlook, has not only looked to Europe but also to the US in common with many, if not most, countries. Gradually, the US has become the leading country for student exchanges and research collaborations but the US has not taken over to the exclusion of European countries. While Singapore has developed truly global research collaborations across the whole research spectrum, Europe still features very strongly. Within Europe, the UK has had a historical advantage. A number of countries feature in Singapore's collaborative portfolios notably with France, Germany and Sweden. Indeed several of these collaborations, such as that with Sweden, are now a couple of decades old. If we look at student preferences for exchange, which also reflects the attraction of existing links in research collaboration, then, at NTU for example, apart from the strong natural attraction of the US and the UK, Sweden is amongst the first choices for both inward and outward exchanges being equal with the US, a little ahead of the UK and well ahead of France and Germany.

This collaboration started with Singapore sending students to European, especially UK, universities for their first degree education and many then stayed to complete their research degrees there. Naturally, collaboration stems from this deeply embedded relationship. With the rise of Singapore as a research centre of excellence, there has been an evolution of the collaborative relationship into one between equals matching research strengths for mutual advantage. In addition, the policy in Singapore of a fourfold recruitment process has also been very influential. Singapore has attracted senior researchers to kick-start research groups and catapult the country into a forefront position in specific priority areas for the nation. It has been able to recruit research "superstars" by its ability to offer a stable and well-funded environment based on an excellent research infrastructure. The second level of recruitment has been to attract the brightest young researchers from across the world which will provide a continuing level of excellence into the future. Finally, Singapore has sought, through various schemes, to attract leading institutions from across the world but significantly from leading European research universities. The CREATE scheme mentioned above is a particularly successful example of bringing such institutions working closely with NUS and NTU.

Examples include MIT and Berkeley from the US, Technion from Israel and, from Europe, ETH Zurich, the Technical University of Munich (TUM), based on its existing presence in the country, and Cambridge University.

As mentioned above, there is also the strong partnership with Imperial College London in the new NTU Medical School and other joint projects between both NUS and NTU with many European academic institutions including Karolinska Institutet, Stockholm (Sweden) and the University of Manchester (UK) and research performing organisations such as CNRS in France, the Fraunhofer Gesellschaft, the German Aerospace Centre (Germany) and the Danish Hydrological Institute. Finally, with its strong academic and research base, Singapore has been able to attract leading high technology multinational corporations by anchoring them through research collaborations between them and the universities. Interestingly, most of these high-level industrial collaborations involve European-based multinationals such as Airbus, Bosch, BMW, Siemens, Rolls-Royce and THALES. It is noteworthy that the EU, through such companies, is by far and away the largest source of inward investment to the Singapore economy.

This has been a two decade long success story for Singapore in terms of its bilateral collaboration. However, a different picture emerges when one considers multilateral collaboration and networking and this is especially relevant when one looks at activities driven at the European level. The value of research networks, a critical development within Europe which has turned its apparent diversity weakness into a strength through networking, has not yet been fully appreciated in Singapore. This is now changing as the world becomes more interconnected and such networking becomes a global rather than a European norm. Singapore has signed a cooperation agreement with the European Molecular Biology Organization (EMBO) and it has also joined the intercontinental collaboration — the Human Frontier Science Programme Organisation. In relation to EU-funded programmes, the situation is more complex although it should hopefully become easier when the comprehensive EU-Singapore Free Trade Agreement, initialled in 2014, comes into force. Singapore, as an advanced economy with a substantial research activity, is in the same group as countries such as the US, Canada, Japan and Australia and so is unable to benefit financially from the Framework programmes (now Horizon 2020). However, investigators from Singapore are able to be co-Principal Investigators and to benefit from being part of well-funded and advanced research networks. Where Singapore researchers have benefitted from EU-funded programmes is in terms of individual mobility awards such as Erasmus Mundus and Marie Sklodowska-Curie awards — schemes that have been open to the whole world and not just Europe.

Within these European programmes, the key development has been the creation of the European Research Council (ERC) operating on the basis of excellence without regard to collaborative requirements within Europe. The ERC's most successful scheme has been that of the Starter Grants for young researchers based on its precursor — the European Science Foundation (ESF) European Young Investigator Awards (EURYI). Now the Starter Grant scheme is open to researchers from across the world provided that the research is carried out principally in a European host institution. With its rapid development and its own commitment to excellence, it is hardly surprising that researchers from within the Singaporean system are now responding to this funding opportunity. Young researchers who have held EURYI awards or Starter Grants are now seeking to continue their careers in Singapore either as successful competitors in the Singaporean version of the scheme (the National Research Foundation Fellowships) or in other funded positions. This demonstrates the attractiveness of the Singaporean research environment, not just in terms of the funding available but with access to research infrastructure and working in a milieu with its two major research universities committed to excellence. This is against a background of Singapore being a truly global city, its respect for the "rule of law", its status as the first-ranked country for competitiveness and as a place to do business and the general attractiveness of life in the city-state.

Singapore has now fully embraced the concept of the knowledge-based economy and put this into effect through a Government that really "walks the talk". While Europe and the European Union in particular have also declared that its economy has to be a knowledge-based one, so far its implementation has been at best patchy. So now Singapore collaborates with Europe and its constituent nations on a basis of equality whereas previously there was somewhat of an "inferiority complex" in its research relationships. Today, the situation is one of equals in many respects, although geographically it is a case of "David and Goliath", and so research collaboration is likely to be more interesting and sustainable. However, in this rapidly globalising world, Europe with its older established states and economies and the new states of the EU's expansion, and Singapore can together provide a substantial, dramatic and increasing contribution to the world's knowledge bank by working together.

Professor Bertil Andersson is President of the Nanyang Technological University and Tony Mayer is the Europe Representative, Nanyang Technological University.

Engineering the Future: Academic Excellence between Germany and Singapore

Contribution from TUM Asia
(Technische Universität München Asia)

Introduction

As we celebrate 50 years of Singapore's independence, we also celebrate the 50 years of friendship between Germany and Singapore. On top of the political, social and economic ties that the two countries enjoy, one additional connection has been made in the last 12 years — a technological exchange of knowledge in the academic field. Both Germany and Singapore are known to have excellent academic institutions that produce some of the best talents worldwide. How much further can we take innovation and science with a collaborative effort between the two powerhouses? The branch campus of the Technische Universität München (TUM) seeks to answer this question.

German Excellence Coming to Asia

Helping to foster a pool of talent in Asia was the purpose and aim of the Technische Universität München (Technical University of Munich, TUM) Asia all along. "The step to take TUM into Asia was something unheard of — no other German university had attempted it before. It was uncharted terrain," said Professor Dr. Wolfgang A. Herrmann, TUM's President.

Founded in 1868 by Bavarian King Ludwig II, TUM is known to be an institute that produces world-changing technologies, with 13 Nobel Prize Laureates to date. When TUM was invited by the Economic Development Board (EDB), Singapore under the Global Schoolhouse Initiative to set up a campus in Singapore, Professor Herrmann — the longest-running university president in Germany and one of the most cited German chemists today — saw it as a natural extension of

TUM's long-time commitment to train the brightest minds in Science and Technology with innovation and contribution to society in mind.

As a visionary leader, Professor Herrmann himself taught in the joint TUM-NUS Master of Science (MSc) in Industrial Chemistry programme in its initial few years. Since then, he has seen an extraordinary strengthening of relations between Germany and Singapore through TUM Asia.

With the concept of global schoolhouse in mind, TUM Asia allows for unique exchanges in cultural and technical knowledge between Europe and Singapore due to the international nature of the teaching between professors and students. In a natural progression, TUM Asia saw the need to also add undergraduate programmes under its belt. Today, TUM Asia offers both standalone and joint Bachelor & Master programmes in Singapore together with partner universities such as the National University of Singapore (NUS), Nanyang Technological University (NTU) and Singapore Institute of Technology (SIT).

Education that Transcends Boundaries

The best way to ensure that "German Engineering" excellence is transferred beyond Europe and into Asia is to fly the teaching staff from TUM to Singapore. In addition, this initiative also allows the German teaching staff to be exposed to the international level of teaching.

"Singapore is a 13-hour flight away from my home in Munich and I teach for at least two weeks at a time. What makes me do it? It is the exciting and interesting atmosphere that gives me new insights. Students come from different Asian countries, bringing a truly unique perspective into the programme," said Professor Ulf Schlichtmann, head of TUM's Institute for Electronic Design Automation Institute in the department of Electrical and Computer Engineering. "They help us as professors gain new insights and enrich our European perspectives. The learning goes both ways."

"What my professors imparted to me was a love for learning," said Lee Poh Sein, valedictorian of the pioneer cohort of Bachelor of Science (BSc) in Chemical Engineering. "Despite knowing that they have an 8-hour lecture ahead of them, they have never compromised on the level of teaching even when fighting jetlag."

Students who come through TUM Asia's programmes have also commended the broad-based curriculum, a characteristic that allows TUM Asia to stand out from the crowd. Nurhidayah Basri chanced upon the joint NUS-TUM MSc Programme in Industrial Chemistry while searching for postgraduate degrees. As she is a Singaporean who had never studied abroad, the opportunity to be taught by TUM professors, plus the prospect of working in Europe, really stood out to her.

Nurhidayah went on to secure an internship and did her thesis in Europe, working in Clariant, a Swiss speciality chemicals company, which to her was "a life-changing experience that prepared [her] to take on new challenges".

Industry-relevant Professors

With a plethora of professors across the globe, what makes TUM's professors highly appreciated to the mix of academics in Singapore? TUM's professors are among the best in their fields and have in common many years of valuable industry experience, hailing from diverse backgrounds as TUM attracts talent across Europe and beyond.

This quality is recognised by students in Singapore. "The modules prepare us adequately for the industry, with the techniques and programmes we learn based on what companies today use. Our professors also use real problems that they face in the industry as tutorial questions for us," mentioned Goh Zhe Liang, a graduate from TUM's BSc programme in Chemical Engineering offered at TUM Asia.

This knowledge is also pronounced in the lessons that TUM Asia students attend. "The programme helped me to understand the finer nuances of my subject of interest, Aerospace Engineering. To be tutored by professors with industry experience and considerable knowledge is not something one can find in all universities. I have learnt from the best in the field," said Somen Bhudolia, a graduate from the joint TUM-NTU MSc in Aerospace Engineering programme. Somen replicated the infectious passion from his professors with an achievement of two international conference papers as a researcher at Nanyang Technological University, where he currently works.

Similarly, the professors benefit from this exchange of academic activity. In 2006, Professor Schlichtmann was invited to establish the joint NTU-TUM MSc Programme in Integrated Circuit Design. Since then, he has seen numerous opportunities available for European companies to tap into top Asian talent equipped with a European-styled education. In 2009, Professor Schlichtmann and his team launched TUM's BSc in Electrical Engineering and Information Technology in partnership with the Singapore Institute of Technology. Today, he travels to Singapore two to five times a year, teaching in the Bachelor and Master programmes and also holding project meetings with companies and research institutes.

Strong Industry Network

TUM's presence in Singapore has also benefitted various industry players. Singapore is home to many multinational companies and corporations, being especially attractive as regional headquarters for companies looking to penetrate the massive Asian market. Today, Singapore is home to numerous European companies, among them over 1,400 companies from Germany.

From the start, TUM Asia has had no difficulty integrating into the local industry landscape. Adopting the TUM model — a practical and innovation-based curriculum in cooperation with the industrial giants surrounding Munich — TUM Asia started its operations in 2002 with strong partnerships forged with companies such as BASF, Budenheim and Clariant. As the years progressed, new programmes were added and their curricula were established in consultation with industry partners, ensuring relevance to the needs of companies.

Through this unique model, TUM Asia established an extensive network of industrial partners from the aerospace, chemical, logistics and semiconductor industries around the world, here in the heart of Asia. On this model, companies have also given their stamp of approval. Mr. Ulf Schneider, Managing Director of Lantiq Asia Pacific, a fabless semiconductor company from Germany, and President of the Singapore Semiconductor Industry Association (SSIA), reflects that "As a driving sector of Singapore's economy, our companies are always on the lookout for technically skilled and global-ready trained engineers. Our collaboration with TUM Asia prepares graduates to become key contributors to the semiconductor companies in Singapore and Asia."

Wong Kye Howe, a graduate with an MSc in Integrated Circuit Design, was formerly sponsored by Lantiq Asia Pacific to study at TUM Asia and he too has benefitted from the learning culture: "The diverse student backgrounds, available scholarships with renowned tech giants and the reputation of TUM made the degree programme very valuable for both the graduates and for employers." Kye Howe was hired by Lantiq Asia Pacific shortly after graduation. Because of the understanding imparted to him during his studies, Kye Howe found the assimilation into a German company smooth.

The successful integration of hundreds of young talents into key industries and companies is something employers can rely on. TUM Asia is a valuable resource for thriving companies looking for staff, in the Asian market, who are enabled with a sensitive understanding of European culture and concepts.

Beyond Education

Besides strong academic programmes and time-tested industrial relationships, TUM and TUM Asia in particular also saw themselves as agents to promote the internationalisation of research capabilities with a twofold purpose: to benefit young countries with an increasing need for R&D competencies and to equip Europeans with the ability to take research out of home ground. This saw the establishment of TUM CREATE, a joint research institution between Technische Universität München (TUM) and Nanyang Technological University (NTU), with funding by the National Research Foundation of Singapore (NRF), an agency of the Prime Minister's Office (PMO).

Since its inception, TUM CREATE (Campus for Research Excellence and Technological Enterprise) has become a full-fledged research body comprising more than 100 scientists, engineers and designers from 20 different countries, working on over 10 research projects. At CREATE, which houses other research groups from universities across three continents (located in NUS U-Town) TUM CREATE boasts an international mix of researchers from TUM and NTU, working together to realise visions of the future — another demonstration of the cross-cultural capabilities between Germany and Singapore.

Moreover, TUM Asia students have the opportunity to participate in the cutting-edge research through their projects and thesis work. Two demonstrators have been completed at TUM CREATE, with the key output termed EVA, which is the first electric vehicle specifically designed as a taxi for tropical megacities. EVA was built from the ground up, moving from concept to prototype in just two years and was unveiled at the Tokyo Motor Show in 2013.

2015 and Beyond: German Roots Firmly Planted in Asia

With the rise of globalisation and rapidly advancing economies, Asia is no longer playing catch-up to the traditional superpowers of the West. As a complex of maturing and emerging economies Asia needs the ability to solve issues on both national and regional levels by having competent and knowledgeable workforces. TUM Asia is here to help equip Asian talents by tapping on the transfer of expertise between Asia and Europe.

In view of worldwide topics of concern such as global warming and a depleting supply of fossil fuels around the world, countries have been emphasising environmental friendliness and sustainability. In 2010, the European Commission proposed a 10-year strategy, Europe 2020, to promote sustainable and inclusive growth. As of 2014, Germany leads the EU for renewable energy production. Emerging industries include energy management, sustainable engineering and renewable energy, all of which are exceptionally important for sustainable growth.

TUM Asia recognised these key topics as potential concerns for Asia and has led the change in the region by tapping on TUM's expertise in developing relevant programmes to train talent in Asia to combat these challenges. On such initiatives, TUM Asia has found supportive partners. One of them is the DAAD, the German Academic Exchange Service. "DAAD awards scholarships to TUM Asia students with outstanding academic results and strong moral character, highlighting the importance of international academic exchange and collaboration between Germany and Singapore. TUM Asia is a strategic scientific partner for Singapore as its programmes emanate TUM's German quality according to the needs of Singapore's growing economy," affirmed the DAAD Information Centre Singapore.

TUM Asia also plans to help foster more entrepreneurial spirit by planning joint degrees with Singaporean partners in the fields of entrepreneurship and technology transfer. The success of TUM Asia's initiatives will be important to the industry on the whole. On the strong and continual partnership between Germany and Singapore, Assistant Managing Director of EDB Mr. Alvin Tan said, "We are very honoured that Singapore was chosen by TUM as the only location outside of Germany to establish an academic and research presence. TUM Asia has forged strong partnerships with leading companies and universities to offer a wide spectrum of programmes that develop technology-oriented talent for industry. We look forward to deepening this partnership in the years ahead."

Irish Connections — Ireland's Intrepid Educationalists in Singapore

Rosemary Lim

On 23 November 2014 Irish-Singaporean, Sister Deirdre O'Loan, received the Public Service Star from President Tony Tan Keng Yam in recognition of her outstanding contribution to education in Singapore. Although Sister Deirdre, an Infant Jesus (IJ) Sister, is not the first Irish teaching missionary to receive this accolade, she will almost certainly be the last. After more than 160 years of contributing to education in Singapore, Irish teaching missionaries here now number just one.

The early history of Ireland's intrepid educationalists in this region is linked with the French Sisters of St. Maur (the IJ Order) and the De La Salle Institute, both founded in the 17th century. Because good English was a much-prized skill in the British Empire, Ireland was an obvious recruiting ground for Catholic teaching missionaries when Father Beurel sought help in setting up schools in Singapore in the mid-19th century. The first Irish and French teaching missionaries arrived here in 1852, when St. Joseph's Institution (SJI) was established. The IJ Sisters, who arrived with the Brothers, continued to Penang where they founded their first school outside France. Two years later, in 1854, more Sisters arrived and the Convent of the Holy Infant Jesus (CHIJ) was opened in Victoria Street. In 1909 a convent was established in Ireland at Drishane, County Cork, with the main purpose of preparing Irish Sisters for work abroad.

Over the next 160 years teaching missionaries of many nationalities taught in Singapore — French, English, German, Belgian, Canadian — as well as Singaporeans, who in turn have gone overseas to share their educational skills. However, the largest national group came from Ireland and for some Singaporeans the word "Irish" is almost synonymous with teacher.

Marymount Convent School was also founded by Irish missionaries, Mother Liguori Bourke and Sister Alphonsus Moody of the Good Shepherd Order, who arrived in Singapore in 1939. A later arrival, Sister Ita Cleere, was the last Irish Good Shepherd Sister in Singapore. Maris Stella High School was set up by the Marist Brothers, among them Brother Kevin Doheny who had already spent over 20 years in Asia before he arrived in Singapore in 1964. Both Sister Ita and Brother Kevin became Singapore citizens and ended their days in their adopted country.

Brother Kevin was one of the Irish missionaries interviewed by the Oral History Centre of the National Archives of Singapore as part of their education project in the 1980s and 1990s. Sister Damien Peggy Murphy, a former principal of CHIJ in Victoria Street and Brother Joseph McNally were also interviewed. Brother McNally's vision for the Arts in Singapore saw the setting up of the De La Salle School of the Arts (see page 139). He was a good friend of Sister Deirdre and she describes his contribution as transformative, ahead of his period and one that has enriched another facet of education in Singapore.

In 2007, aware that the numbers of Irish teaching missionaries in Singapore were dwindling, an Irish resident here initiated a second oral history project to record the stories of the few that remained. Sister Deirdre, a former principal of Catholic Junior College, was the first interviewee of this new project. Another interviewee was Sister Elizabeth Browne, the last Irish principal of CHIJ Victoria Street before its move to Toa Payoh in 1983. She spent "a very happy 27 years in Singapore" before moving back to Ireland. In her interview she recalled that pupils always wanted to deal with difficult work and demanded to have homework.

De La Salle Brother Patrick Oliver Rogers left Ireland in 1954 to teach in Malaysia. He came to Singapore during 1977 and taught the last A Level classes at St. Patrick's School, where he was principal for a year until ill health meant he returned to the classroom at SJI in 1984 when the late Brother Kevin Byrne was principal, the last Irish Brother to hold that role. SJI moved from Bras Basah Road to Malcolm Road during this time. After retirement, Brother Oliver began organising the neglected Lasallian archives in Singapore and Petaling Jaya, with some documents dating from the 19th century. These were so brittle and tattered that the National Archives of Singapore offered to microfilm them, preserving the records for the future. Brother Oliver returned to Ireland in 2004 and continues to work on the archives in Ireland at the Castletown monastery where most of the Irish Brothers began their training as novices leading eventually to their journeys as teaching missionaries.

Other De La Salle Brothers interviewed for the project were the late Brothers Joseph Kiely and Senan Bergin. Marc Nerva, past president of the Irish Graduates Association of Singapore (IGAS), attended De La Salle schools from 1988 to 1997, first St. Stephen's then St. Patrick's. Although most of the Irish Brothers had retired from teaching by the time Marc reached secondary school, their influence still remained. "Lasallian boys are very recognisable because of the influence of the Irish Brothers on us and the unrivalled spirit they have left us with," says Marc. He remembers Brother Kevin Byrne, his Spiritual Director at St. Patrick's, and knew Brother Senan Bergin. Brother Joseph Kiely also visited Singapore during those years. "I always looked forward to his articles in our school yearbooks and newsletters," says Marc, a finance and HR manager. He continues:

> Generations of boys who passed through the halls of the various Lasallian institutions in Singapore have shaken their school walls with proud and thunderous renditions of our schools' common rally. Little do many of us realise, though, that our rally is based on an Irish marching song entitled O'Donnell Abú. Many of us sang this song for 10 years. Many of us still find ourselves singing and stirred by it today.

Marc's contact with Irish educationalists did not end when he left St. Patrick's. In 2008 he graduated from University College Dublin (UCD) with a BSc in Finance in a Singapore-based programme. So while the Irish educational legacy in primary and secondary education is being carried on by Singaporeans, other Singaporeans are establishing and continuing links with Ireland through tertiary education.

IGAS members include Irish and Singaporeans. A former president is Dr. Stanley Quek, who was also Honorary Consul General for Ireland in Singapore from 1993 until 2001. An Honorary Fellow of Trinity College Dublin (TCD), from where he graduated with a medical degree in 1972, Dr. Quek points out that "Ireland is not only English speaking, but has one of the highest educated workforces in the world." In 2013, in a special ceremony held at the Irish Residence in Singapore, Dr. Quek was conferred an honorary Doctorate in Medicine from the National University of Ireland to coincide with the 25th Anniversary celebrations of the formation of the Irish Universities and Medical Schools Consortium "in whose success in South-East Asia Stanley Quek has played a leading role".

Other Singaporean medical graduates from Ireland's top institutions include two married couples, MP Dr. Lily Neo and her husband Dr. Ben Neo, and Dr. Ivy Yap and her husband Dr. Leslie Lam, a Lasallian old boy and an Honorary Fellow of UCD. Their links with Ireland have been strong and continuous.

Dr. Lam is also a board member of the Singapore Ireland Fund (TSIF), an Institution of Public Character. Dr. Quek, the board chairman, says the fund "illustrates the long and historical relationship that exists between Singapore and Ireland". It promotes Singapore-Ireland links through educational philanthropy, such as the Singapore Ireland Fund Overseas Immersion Programme Grant, an endowment fund set up to provide four annual scholarships for Physiotherapy or Occupational Therapy students from the Singapore Institute of Technology who will complete their degree courses at TCD. So although one era of Singapore-Irish educational exchange is coming to an end, others have begun and will continue to grow.

According to the great Irish writer George Bernard Shaw, "Progress is impossible without change." Change and progress go hand-in-hand as far as Sister Deirdre is concerned. Innovations in Singapore's education during the 50 years since 1965 include the setting up of Junior Colleges. Sister Deirdre came to Singapore to teach at Catholic Junior College (CJC), having spent more than a decade at Bukit Nanas Convent in Kuala Lumpur. In 1994 she retired as principal of CJC and took up her present role as supervisor of the 11 CHIJ schools in Singapore. The first formal CHIJ Board of Management was set up in 1975, chaired by Dr. Ee Peng Liang. Since then an IJ Sister has been supervisor, providing support and encouragement, guidance and advice both to the board and to the CHIJ schools.

Twenty years on, and 56 years after she first left Ireland, Sister Deirdre has overseen the introduction of new ideas and improvements, including the rebuilding of all the CHIJ schools. She continues to be extremely interested in the development of education in Singapore. Her regular school visits mean she is up to date with their latest news, projects and events. "Each school is similar in ethos but distinctive thanks to the history that has shaped it." Though no longer in the classroom, Sister Deirdre is familiar to CHIJ girls through her visits, writing for school newsletters and yearbooks, as well as giving speeches on special occasions.

In describing her role, Sister Deirdre speaks of fidelity to the original vision of the IJ Sisters, the traditions of the CHIJ schools and re-interpreting these for the needs of education today. "I am enthusiastic about changes and developments in Singapore's education. The system has been transformed with multiple pathways and possibilities," she says. Being open to transformation, looking for new ideas, new approaches and methodologies in teaching, without losing sight of the IJ legacy and essential vision, are among the reasons why the CHIJ schools have survived and continue to thrive for over a century-and-a-half.

Preparing for the future is something that Sister Deirdre embraces. For the past few years a number of the management tasks connected with the supervisor's role has been shared with a lay person, while she keeps a watching brief on the important thrust of ongoing formation. "As a retiree I am well placed to do the work, so long as I have the mental powers and enthusiasm," she adds.

Singapore is now home for Sister Deirdre. "I will always remain Irish," she says, "but I have put down roots here and I have wonderful friends. Singapore adopted me rather than I adopted Singapore."

And what does Ireland think of her sons and daughters who have contributed so much in foreign lands? For many Irish it means an instant connection wherever they go in the world. Even today Sister Deirdre, now in her early 80s, helps new arrivals settle in to Singapore, people she does not know but who are referred to her through friends and relatives in Ireland. New arrivals may also feel an affinity with Singapore because of their own missionary relatives. Cormac Hynes of the Irish embassy takes pride in his great-uncle, Brother Aloysius Sweeney, who taught at SJI in the 1950s and was a contemporary and childhood neighbour of Brother McNally. No doubt there are Josephians in Singapore who remember him, perhaps even President Tony Tan Keng Yam, who attended both St. Patrick's and SJI.

The final words come from President Michael D. Higgins of Ireland who sent a letter of congratulations to Sister Deirdre, acknowledging and celebrating her outstanding contribution to the people of Singapore in the field of education. He wrote: "It reminds us [the Irish] of the role that our religious communities have played as educators, providing new possibilities for young people all over the world."

References

Brown, F. (1997). *La Salle Brothers, Malaya & Singapore, 1852–1952*. Petaling Jaya: Lasallian Publications.

Browne, E. (2008). Oral History Interview, 4 April 2008. Interviewed by Lim, R. Accession Number: 003296. National Archives of Singapore.

Catholic News. (2013). History of the Good Shepherd Sisters in S'pore. Retrieved 19 December 2014 from http://www.catholicnews.sg/index.php?option=com_content&view=article&id=9534:history-of-the-good-shepherd-sisters-in-spore&catid=355:december-15-2013-vol-63-no-25&Itemid=473.

Chua, A. (2011). Tony Tan Keng Yam. Retrieved 2 January 2015 from http://eresources.nlb.gov.sg/infopedia/articles/SIP_1846_2011-10-13.html.

Hynes, C. (2014). *RE: Singapore Students in Ireland,* e-mail to Lim, R. 15 December [29 December 2014].

Kong, L. et al. (1994). *Convent Chronicles*. Singapore: Armour.

Lam, L. (2014). Profile. Retrieved 2 January 2015 from http://leslielam.com.sg/profile.htm.

Lim, R. (2008). *An Irish Tour of Singapore*. Singapore: Two Trees.

Murphy, M. (2013). Text of the Introductory Address Delivered by Dr. Michael B. Murphy, President, University College Cork on 13 March 2013 in the Irish Residence, Singapore, on the Occasion of the Conferring of the Degree of Medicine, *honoris causa*, on Stanley Swee Han Quek. Retrieved 18 December 2014 from http://www.nui.ie/college/docs/citations/2013/quek.pdf.

National University of Ireland. (2013). NUI Honours Dr. Stanley Quek. Retrieved 18 December 2014 from http://www.nui.ie/news/2013/quekHonCon.asp.

Nerva, M. (2014). *Re: Irish Ambassador's Request for SG50 Book Essay*, e-mail to Lim, R. 16 December [29 December 2014].

O'Hara, L. (2014, November 30). Friends, Ex-Students Pay Tribute to late SJI Principal at Mass. *Catholic News*, p. 9.

O'Loan, D. (2014). Interviewed by: Lim, R. (17 December 2014).

—— (2014) *Re: Essay Draft*, e-mail to Lim, R. 22 December [29 December 2014].

Quek, S. (2014). *Re: Irish Ambassador's Request for SG50 Book Essay*, e-mail to Lim, R. 15 December [29 December 2014].

Rogers, O. (2008). Oral History Interview, 21 October 2008. Interviewed by Lim, R. Accession Number: 002889. National Archives of Singapore.

Singapore Institute of Technology. (2013). The Singapore Ireland Fund Overseas Immersion Programme Grant. Retrieved 18 December 2014 from http://www.singaporetech.edu.sg/tuition-fees/the-singapore-ireland-fund-overseas-immersion-programme-grant-6.

The Ireland Funds. (2009). The Singapore Ireland Fund. Retrieved 18 December 2014 from https://www.theirelandfunds.org/Singapore.

Rosemary Lim is originally from Northern Ireland and has lived in Singapore since 1990. As the author of **An Irish Tour of Singapore** *and a volunteer oral history interviewer of the Irish in Singapore and Malaysia, Rosemary is well placed to write about her fellow-countrymen in this part of the world.*

NUS' Connections with Europe: Our Students' Experience with European Partners

Anne Pakir

Introduction

"We must therefore give even higher priority at NUS, to helping our students develop as well-rounded individuals, with the crucial personal qualities of: Inquisitiveness; Initiative; Inner Resilience; Imagination; Inclusiveness and Integrity. As these attributes, quite coincidentally, all start with "I", I will refer to them collectively as i-NUS qualities."

Tan Chorh Chuan,
President, National University of Singapore,
State of the University Address 2013

At 110 years old, the National University of Singapore (NUS) is known today for its high quality, internationally-oriented education which allows its undergraduates to undertake global learning journeys within and beyond Singaporean classrooms.

In helping to build the nation's human capital, NUS seeks to nurture individuals who frequently ask questions rather than just absorb knowledge, and are well-rounded in mind and character. The students are nudged into becoming global citizens, sensitive to and effective in diverse cultural settings. They are expected to be resourceful and enterprising, with the NUS i-qualities of inquisitiveness, inner resilience, imagination, inclusiveness and integrity.

Many of the NUS i-qualities are being developed through meaningful and structured broad-based global educational programmes such as the NUS Overseas Colleges (NOCs), the Student Exchange Programme (SEP), and Double, Joint or Concurrent Degree programmes jointly offered with prestigious foreign university partners. Overseas educational programmes such as the International Summer

Programme (i-SP), International Internships (i-Intern), International Research Attachments (i-RAP) and Study Trips for Engagement and EnRichment (STEER) are popular with students. Currently, NUS has 300 University-wide and Faculty-level SEP partner universities in 50 countries, 6 NOCs in 5 countries, and about 30 joint, double and concurrent degree programmes with overseas partners. Many of these thriving partnerships are with European universities.

But first we have to ask the question, "What is Europe?" Our distinguished Ambassador-at-Large, Professor Tommy Koh responded well and to the point in 2003: "I see Europe as a concept based on geography, history, culture, economy, common political values and legal tradition, and a shared vision." Europe is geographically "all the lands stretching from the Urals to the Atlantic, and from the Arctic to the Mediterranean Sea." Europe is seen historically as "the source of our colonial domination from the 18th to the 20th centuries." For example, we find British, French, Dutch, Portuguese and Spanish colonisers in Southeast Asia. Melaka (Malacca) was a Portuguese colony for 130 years (1511–1641) before the Dutch arrived, and after the latter, the British.

Europe is also "an exemplar of modernity".[1] During the emergent years of independence and sovereignty, in the past two centuries, "Asian intellectuals looked to Europe for ideas on how to modernise their societies." Europe, Ambassador Koh reminds us, offered exciting notions of "secularism, science and technology, industrialisation, democracy and the ideal of progress". Finally, many people are attracted by European civilisation, a high culture, epitomised in Dante and Shakespeare, Beethoven and Verdi, da Vinci and Picasso, Newton and Darwin, Socrates and Descartes, Marx and Weber, Wittgenstein and Kant, Adam Smith and Maynard Keynes.

When we contrast the vastly different geopolitical, sociocultural and economic landscapes of a huge and old continent like Europe against a tiny, modern city-state republic like Singapore, with its 50 years of independence, we immediately see the value of cultural and educational immersions of students in each other's higher education environments.

Trends in Student Mobility

Student mobility programmes have become an integral part of the higher education landscape in Singapore. Singaporean students no longer choose their preferred higher education institution based solely on the academic programmes offered. Their choices are very much influenced by the study abroad opportunities offered by the institution. For students who have made a deliberate decision to study in a

---

[1] Tommy Koh, "Learning from Europe," in *Desperately Seeking Europe*, eds. S. Stern and E. Seligmann (London: Archetype Publications 2003), 67–71.

Singapore university instead of overseas, the prospect of having "the best of both worlds" (study for a degree in Singapore with the opportunity to spend time abroad for an exchange programme) becomes even more desirable. Recognising this trend, NUS has devoted much of its resources to developing quality mobility programmes for its students. The target is to provide 70% of NUS undergraduates with at least one study abroad experience during their candidature.

The Student Exchange Programme (SEP) is the flagship and largest global programme in NUS, with about 2,000 NUS students participating in one- or two-semester exchange at a partner university each year. In return, NUS hosts an equal number of students on its campus. NUS started SEP with European universities in 1997 with only seven partner universities. The number of partner universities for SEP increased rapidly over the years and by 2008, NUS had almost 90 partner universities in Europe across 20 countries. From 1997 to 2007, NUS would typically have hosted more students from Europe than it would have sent out. From 2008, however, the trend was reversed, with more NUS students participating in SEP to European universities than the number of European students received by NUS. This possibly reflects a change in the perception of Europe by students in NUS. Today, 50% of NUS students who participate in SEP go to Europe, compared to 28% to the Americas and 22% to Asia and Australasia.

Developing Strategic Partnerships

The focus of collaborations with European universities in the earlier days was restricted to student exchange. Through the years, as relationships with the partner universities deepen, the partnerships have expanded beyond SEP and become more multifaceted. This could be attributed to European institutions generally viewing NUS as a compatible partner. The European Union (EU) also sees Singapore as an important partner to further relations with as evidenced by the setting up of the EU Centre in Singapore to serve the Southeast Asian region.

Building on complementary strengths in curriculum, research and industry links, NUS has co-developed academic programmes, research collaborations, faculty exchanges and other collaborations with top European universities. Some of these flagship initiatives include the Double Degree Programme with six French Grandes Ecoles, Concurrent Degree Programmes with King's College London, Joint Masters of Science with the Technical University of Munich and Joint PhD with Imperial College London, King's College London and the University of Edinburgh. NUS has also set up an Overseas College in Stockholm, partnering the Royal Institute of Technology (KTH) in offering a rare opportunity for students to learn entrepreneurship by being immersed in Stockholm's thriving entrepreneurial environment.

Student Mobility in United Kingdom (UK)

Student mobility to the UK started modestly in 1998 with two partner universities, namely, the University of Newcastle and the University of Bristol. To date, approximately 1,400 NUS students have participated in SEP with 17 UK partner institutions. Over the years, the UK has remained a highly popular SEP destination for students due to the strong academic reputation of the institutions, familiarity with the language and its rich culture. Most of NUS' UK partner institutions are members of the UK Russell Group, a congregation of 24 UK universities committed to the highest levels of academic excellence in both teaching and research. In recent years, NUS has also increasingly become a popular destination for UK students to spend an academic semester. This can be attributed to NUS' growing academic reputation, UK universities' active promotion of study abroad programmes as well as NUS' concerted effort in promoting its rigorous academic culture and welcoming campus environment to students in its partner institutions.

Besides reciprocal student exchange, NUS also sends Law majors to the Centre for Transnational Legal Studies (CTLS) in London on a non-reciprocal arrangement. CTLS is a joint venture with the world's most renowned law schools to focus on transnational legal issues in a multicultural and transnational setting. Both King's College and NUS are founding institutions of the CTLS, which is an affiliate of the Georgetown University Law Center in Washington DC.

Imperial College London

Building on the strength of existing academic exchange through SEP, Imperial College and NUS established a Joint Doctor of Philosophy Degree Programme in 2010 to train five to ten graduate students per year in the areas of Computing, Engineering, Medicine and Science. Upon completion of the programme, students would receive a jointly conferred degree from both universities.

To provide Imperial and NUS undergraduate students with early exposure to research, the NUS-Imperial College London Summer International Research Exchange was established to facilitate the exchange of students during the summer. NUS students would conduct research work in an Imperial laboratory under the supervision of a researcher. Similarly, Imperial students would do the same at NUS. Funding from the Santander Bank has been made available to support this research initiative. To date, Imperial has sent close to 40 students to NUS on summer research and NUS has sent close to 25 students to Imperial.

Starting in 2013, NUS students could apply to Imperial's three-week summer school offered by its Business School to take courses in Finance, Strategic Marketing, Business Strategy & Consulting and Innovation & Entrepreneurship. More than 30 students have participated in the summer school.

King's College London

King's and NUS have mutually identified each other as strategic partners. Student exchange with King's started only in 2003 with movement of less than 10 semester exchange students per year. The compatibility in academic calendar and courses and positive exchange experiences in the respective institutions have encouraged the growth in student exchange with numbers growing threefold.

> *"The research culture is strong. Lecturers placed a premium on independent studies and in developing a critical research-oriented thinking. In a somewhat different approach, lecture contact times and module syllabus are less compared to NUS, giving students more time to understand and do reading. This somewhat reminded me of the "teach less learn more" approach touted by Ministry of Education."*
>
> Tan Kok Yong Warren, Faculty of Science,
> on his exchange experience at
> King's College London in Academic Year 2013/14,
> Semester 1

Building on the strong relationship established through SEP, both institutions entered into a Joint PhD programme in the areas of English Literature, History, Geography, Philosophy, Political Science and Sociology in 2010. Shortly after, in 2013, the NUS Faculty of Science established a Joint PhD with King's School of Biomedical Sciences to train graduates in the area of Life Sciences and Biomedical Science.

In order to provide trained manpower in the niche areas of Analytical Toxicology, Forensic Science and Biophysics for the Singapore job market, the NUS Faculty of Science has also established Concurrent Degree Programmes (CDP) with King's School of Biomedical Sciences. These programmes provide a through-train pathway for students from the Bachelor of Science (Honours) programme in NUS to progress to a one-year Master of Science/Master of Research programme in King's. Through this collaboration, NUS students are able to gain access to the highly sought after Master's programmes in King's. Students who wish to explore if the research environment in King's is suitable for them before committing to a graduate programme are able to do so by participating in research programmes during the summer under the supervision of a faculty member.

For students who want to have a taste of the academic environment in King's, the University offers summer schools with courses in Arts, Literature & Culture, Business & Management, Health & Society, Latin & Ancient Greek, Law, Natural & Mathematical Sciences, Politics & Social Sciences, as well as a range of unique courses which are taught in collaboration with famous London institutions such as the Victoria & Albert Museum, the United Nations High Commission for

Refugees, the Museum of London and the Royal United Services Institute. About 60 students participated in the summer school in 2014.

Much has been done to promote student mobility between the two institutions. In 2008, King's and NUS each offered an annual Partnership Award that enables a member of staff at each university to spend time at the partner institution. This award has promoted closer research collaborations between researchers from both institutions.

Student Mobility in France

NUS collaborates with more than 20 top institutions in France through academic programmes, many of which started before the year 2000. Collaborations with French institutions range widely from academic programmes to research collaborations. NUS also continuously seeks to create and enhance partnerships with leading French institutions that provide quality academic and unique French cultural exposure to NUS students, apart from contributing to the research vibrancy at NUS.

Through SEP partnerships with French institutions, NUS students have the opportunities to experience the French higher education system and gain knowledge of French culture and language. Students participating in SEP spend one or two semesters at one of NUS' 19 French partner institutions while NUS hosts students from French partner institutions on the NUS campus in return. To encourage more students to participate in SEP to France and to alleviate the anxiety of not knowing the language, the Language Preparation Programme (LPP) for French language administered by the NUS Centre for Language Studies (CLS) was developed in year 2000. In addition, the French Language Immersion Award (LIA) was introduced to sponsor students for the Language Immersion Programme in France to further improve their French language proficiency. The language preparatory class has played an important role in promoting student mobility to France. To date, over 1,000 students have participated in SEP through partnerships between NUS and French partner institutions. Both incoming students from French partner institutions and NUS students have shared positive feedback on their exchange semesters at the respective host institutions.

> *"I had an amazing five months of exchange there in Centrale and in Paris. Paris is really beautiful and very rich in culture and history... The sheer volume of museums is like there are endless treasures in just one vault. Walking down the streets of Paris is like walking through centuries to witness the evolution of Western civilisation. I have made many new friends and we had a great time together in Europe. We have travelled to many different places, seen various cultures sharing and creating, tried out delicious local food, and appreciated the great work of both nature and*

men. It occurred to me that all this experience is a gift to me, for a better and more open-minded person in the future."

*Luo Hao, Faculty of Engineering,
on his SEP experience to the Ecole Centrale Paris
in Academic Year 2013/14*

Over the past decade, partnerships with many French partner institutions have strengthened through better understanding and expansion of new collaborations. Of special note is the French-NUS Double Degree Programme with a selection of the Grandes Ecoles (FDDP). Some examples of the multifaceted partnerships are as below:

- With INSA Lyon: SEP, Language Immersion Programme, International Research Attachment Programme;
- With the Ecole Superieure d'Electricité (Supélec): French-NUS Double Degree Programme (FDDP), SEP, Joint PhD, Joint Laboratory-SONDRA;
- With Ecole Polytechnique: FDDP, International Research Attachment Programme;
- With Sciences Po Paris: SEP, Double Degree Programme for Master in Public Policy and Master in Public Affairs.

French universities are re-organising into massive local federations of existing universities and institutes of higher education. The re-organisation effort that was initially known as PRES (Pôle de recherche et d'enseignement supérieur) — higher education and research poles and later as comUE (communautés d'universités et établissements) — aims to enhance international visibility of French Institutions to foster international collaborations.

The re-organisation effort of French institutions has encouraged the expansion of the international partnership of its member institutions' bilateral partnerships to a federation level which includes all other member institutions within the federation. Such expansion of collaboration is well illustrated by the NUS-Sciences Po bilateral partnership which is now enlarged to the collaboration with the Université Paris Sorbonne Cité (USPC) federation. USPC is a higher education and research alliance established in 2010 comprising eight member institutions — four Parisian universities and four higher education and research institutes. The NUS-USPC collaborations started with Sciences Po Paris leading the federation of USPC in 2013. A total of four calls for joint collaborations have been launched within the NUS community and USPC community since then. The NUS-USPC calls for joint collaborations are in the areas of research, graduate and PhD mobility, and education and teaching projects. The first call for research collaboration has seen a total of nine joint research projects awarded funding through the NUS-USPC alliance.

Moving forward, NUS will continue to work with strategic French partner institutions in widening its scope of collaborations. NUS is looking forward to continue engagement with various member institutions of French Higher Education institution federations such as the USPC, Université Paris-Saclay and Sorbonne Universities in areas of common interests to further strengthen the partnerships with French institutions in years to come.

Student Mobility in Germany

Germany has emerged as one of the top most popular SEP destinations for NUS students in recent years. Student exchange with Germany started in 1998 with only one partner university, the Technische Universität München (TUM). Today, NUS has 17 partner institutions in Germany and more than 800 students have gone on exchange to Germany. NUS has also hosted more than 1,000 German students since the inception of SEP with Germany.

There is a steady growth in demand for exchange opportunities to Germany due to the quality education provided by our partner institutions, increase in the number of courses taught in English as well as the rich German culture. The German LPP conducted by the NUS Centre for Language Studies has also fostered the increase in demand. Students having gone through four semesters of language preparation, and spending a month in Germany on a Language Immersion Programme (LIP) would gain greater confidence in handling life in Germany. Many students on the German LIP have benefitted from the support of Deutscher Akademischer Austausch Dienst (DAAD) — Germany's principal agency for the support of international academic cooperation and exchange. Students who go to universities in the State of Baden-Württemberg (BW) can apply for the BW Scholarship. The generous funding from these agencies has helped promote international exchange. Students have responded positively to the exchange experience in Germany.

> *"It is definitely one of the highlights of my university life. I can experience a totally different education system and culture. It is possible to immerse in the Germany culture as a 'local' for four months, which is not possible if you are just travelling to the country as a tourist. In addition, the professors and classmates are very friendly to exchange student, I can get help easily whenever I want. In conclusion, SEP is a life-changing experience definitely not to be missed."*
>
> *Liu Zetong,*
> *Faculty of Engineering,*
> *on her SEP experience to RWTH Aachen, Germany*

TUM was one of NUS' earliest German partner institutions and today, TUM is a strategic partner. As noted elsewhere in this volume, TUM set up the German Institute of Science and Technology (GIST) in Singapore to provide advanced graduate education in technical subjects. NUS partners GIST and TUM in one of GIST's joint degrees, the Master of Science in Industrial Chemistry, which has an enrolment of 20 students each year. The NUS-TUM-GIST Joint Master's programme has a 2-month internship component which can take place in either Europe or Singapore.

Students who wish to experience Germany without spending the whole semester away can choose to participate in summer programmes offered by the University of Ulm and the Ludwig Maximilian University of Munich. Such summer programmes often include the option of an intensive German Language Course. Research-inclined students can also apply for research opportunities during the summer in universities such as the Humboldt University of Berlin, the University of Bonn and the University of Ulm where they would be mentored by world class researchers in the fields of Engineering, Sciences and Technology.

On the research front, since 2007, NUS and Baden-Württemberg have held Joint Scientific Conferences in Life Sciences either in Singapore or in Germany. At these conferences, research findings from joint projects between NUS and German universities researchers in the fields of cancer, genetics and genomics, microbiology, bioengineering, regenerative medicine, drug development, immunology, neurobiology and translational research were presented. Such collaborations have helped Singapore further develop its position as the scientific and education hub of Southeast Asia.

Celebrating Our Connections with Europe

NUS' connections with Europe can be found at all levels: student exchange, academic collaborations and joint research programmes. The focus of this chapter, student mobility between NUS, Singapore and Europe, has provided the scenario of students moving from and to each other's territories in this new century. From the constant exchanges, students from both regions begin to understand "the other", viz. the other's cultural, socioeconomic, historical and educational landscapes, paving the road for deeper and stronger collaborations between our leaders in the future. In time to come, we hope to be able to celebrate further a stronger integration among our students in their understanding of European ideals and Asian realities, or conversely, Asian ideals and European realities. Influencing the future would depend on how our young undergraduates seek and explore beyond their shores, whether from European higher education institutions to NUS or vice versa. They will inherit the mantle of leadership at home and abroad along their multiple paths of growth and development. It is hoped, that with increasing student mobility and through their sharing and exchanges, European and Singaporean students will become imbued with qualities of inquisitiveness, inner resilience, imagination, inclusiveness and integrity, all essential individual and collective attributes, in order for them to face a most challenging 21st century fraught with many global and divisive trials with the greatest promise of success.

Dr. Anne Pakir is the Director of International Relations Office (IRO), National University of Singapore. She is grateful to IRO colleagues Aileen Bong, Chan Mei Mei, Amelia Chang, Koh Li Ling and Yap Wei Lin, for their helpful input.

Section 4

People Matter(s)

Brother Joseph McNally: Son of Ballintubber, Ireland and Singapore

Molly Hennigan and Cheryl Julia Lee

It is early on a foggy Sunday morning in November when we leave the inn for Lough Carra, armed with only a vague idea of where we are headed. Tomas McNally had driven us there the evening before but it was dark and it had been lashing. But it doesn't matter because in Ballintubber there is just that one main road that runs through the town, with little turns on either side into the Abbey, the pub, and the front yards of the townsfolk. We pull our jackets in a little closer to our bodies and look behind us every once in a while for the occasional car and waving driver. At the lake, we see what we have made the trek for — Christ, breaking bread, fishes over the fire. He is looking out over Lough Carra, watching for His fisherman. At His feet, reeds and empty boats, some of which looked like they had been abandoned for a long time. Behind Him, Castle Burke in ruins. It seems appropriate that it begins to drizzle. Feed the multitudes, the Bible says in the parable of the Five Loaves and Two Fishes. This sculpture is our first real introduction to Brother Joseph McNally's work and, as accidents tend to be, it turns out so perfectly apt an encapsulation of who the man was and what his life had been like.

. . . . .

John Joseph McNally was born in 1923 in Ballintubber, a small town in County Mayo in the west of Ireland. At 14, he left to join the La Salle Order of Brothers as an educator. This was a role he went on to live out as his vocation and which brought him to Singapore in 1946. Of the Order he said with pride, "We were teachers, teachers for the rest of our lives." From 1946 to 1983, Brother Joseph taught in Singapore and Malaysia, making brief sojourns to his native Ireland, as well as to New York and Italy to pursue further studies. Alongside this dedication to education, he also nursed a passion for the arts, having grown up in a community where stories were always told around the fireplace, songs always sung, music always played. After retiring in 1983, he merged his two loves by setting up the St. Patrick's Arts Centre, which eventually became LASALLE College of the Arts.[1]

Brother Joseph continues to be defined by his vocation and today, more than a decade after his death in 2002, he is best remembered as a committed teacher who was in equal measure an eager student. "He had a mind that would never go to rest," says his sister, Teresa O'Toole, "and what he learned he was always happy to pass on. He didn't feel it was going to lessen him. He was such a generous man. He would help anyone who approached him and he would always find time he hadn't got."

She stands up and shows us a miniature replica of one of Brother Joseph's sculptures from above the fireplace; it is *Counsellor II*: two bronze figures — a teacher and a student leaning toward each other — and in between them a space for understanding. Teresa asks us if we have seen it before and we nod. Yes, and almost everywhere we have been warmly welcomed into this weekend: in Maura's bed and breakfast where we spend the night, in Tomas' kitchen; later we find it in the expansive grounds of the Turlough Park Estate. It stands, a totem of sorts, testament to Brother Joseph's legacy.

Teresa proudly recalls the people who came up to her during her brother's funeral: "I was amazed. All the people who came up to me had tears in their eyes and said, 'You will never know how much Brother Joseph did for me. He changed my life.' He gave them courage and he gave them confidence."

We nod again as if we are familiar with the man himself. This keeps coming up in our conversations about Brother Joseph, his particular way of making someone feel special and confident. Teresa's daughter, Helen, is someone close to home who benefitted from Brother Joseph's encouragement. A self-conscious girl, Helen was constantly told by her teacher that she was stupid and as a result, left primary school with the idea that she simply wasn't good enough. Two hours with her uncle, during which he encouraged her love for painting and shared his knowledge with her, gave her all the confidence she lacked. "Helen went back to school and flew," says Teresa. "She won herself a scholarship for her first year at college, and put herself through the rest of her time there." After pursuing further studies and a teaching stint at LASALLE College alongside her uncle, Helen is now an accomplished artist and Chair of the Painting and Drawing Program at the University of Washington, Seattle.

More than anything else — talent, circumstances — Brother Joseph believed in grit and work. He believed in the importance of setting a goal and striving towards it.

---

[1] Setting up an arts college is hardly a simple task today, and even less so in the 1980s when the arts were not a priority on the national agenda. Since its founding, LASALLE has quickly risen among the ranks; today it is a partner institution of the prestigious Goldsmiths College in London and was also recently named one of the best art schools across the globe by Spear's, an award-winning European magazine.

In his dealings with students and his artwork, he worked with a clear view to an end goal although the path was not necessarily clear or fixed, and the goal itself could be subject to change.

This embracing of possibilities manifests itself in Brother Joseph's art as well. A painter and a sculptor, he worked with a variety of media and his style was always changing. "He never set out to sculpt a piece into a particular object but rather guided it towards a new shape and existence," says Tom, Teresa's son. "He would pick up on certain aspects of the wood, for example, in which he saw potential and would begin working to uncover that. The art is in the nature; we just enhance it." Brother Joseph worked with art the way he worked with his students; he identified their strengths and built on them until they took on a life of their own. He was an educator who sculpted minds and a sculptor who let himself be educated by his medium. His view was: "Matter's inertia must be given energy. In the same way, people must be given spirit, that is, they must be inspired."[2]

. . . . .

We leave material witnesses when we leave, artists most of all — objects on which are inscribed experiences and our presence. But if we lead our lives with passion and humility, as Brother Joseph certainly did, we might just leave behind a living community which loves and remembers us, and in doing so, keeps our stories alive.

Ballintubber remembers and celebrates Brother Joseph McNally. Today, his larger sculptures stand guard by the entrance to the Abbey and on the shores of Lough Carra, while smaller works and miniature replicas can be found in the homes of his family and friends. His name is spoken with a smile and more often than not, a hand to the heart. But more than these, what brought us closer to the idea of the man was the people of Ballintubber themselves. A portrait of Brother Joseph is a portrait of Ballintubber. In them, we locate the origins and the continuance of Brother Joseph's great spirit: his grace and humour, his generosity and kindness. And his determination. The people of Ballintubber are committed to the painstaking restoration and conservation of their Abbey, the icon and pride of the little town. Built by King Cathal O'Conor in 1216, it is the only still-operational church in Ireland that was founded by an Irish King. Ballintubber Abbey, the Abbey that refuses to die.

> "There's no people in the wide world
> Prouder than the people there
> Of the immortal Abbey to which they are
> The heir."
> — *The Ballad of Ballintubber*

---

[2] As quoted by Bridget Tracy Tan, curator to the exhibition of Brother Joseph's works, "An Invitation to Nature" (2003), held in Dublin.

It is with this same fierce affection with which they protect their cultural heritage, that they guard the memory of their beloved Brother Joseph.

· · · · ·

"I am happy to be Johnny McNally from Ballintubber. I love both Ballintubber, Ireland and Singapore."[3] Brother Joseph loved his hometown and he loved Singapore just as fiercely. "He was so proud of Singapore, of his citizenship," says Tom. "He was going to be buried there. There was no question of that." When Brother Joseph first went over to Singapore, it was far from the world-class country it is today. But as he always did, he saw the potential and did what he could to contribute to its development. In many ways, he took Singapore on as he would a student.

And whether it was imparting the values of independence and tenacity that he learned from his community to his students, or taking on the arduous task of handpicking bogwood from Ireland and having it sent over to Singapore where he turned it into artworks, Brother Joseph's actions always spoke of a desire to bridge the two cultures.

A few weeks after our weekend trip to Ballintubber, we speak to Jacquie Moore and Jenny Deery from the Office of Public Works in Dublin about the exhibition of Brother Joseph's works there, "An Invitation to Nature," and we think about how important it was to the meaning of Brother Joseph's work; although most were completed in Singapore, many of the artworks included in the exhibition had both literal and metaphorical origins in Ireland. The Irish bogwood Brother Joseph used for many of his sculptures was of particular significance; he believed that the ancient bogwood "had been 'incarnated' through the Spirit of God thousands of years ago. It had died, been buried by nature and now it is resurrected through the same spirit into a new beauty."[4] The artworks had finally come home, even if only for the duration of the exhibition. Sadly, Brother Joseph passed away a mere month into the organisation efforts and did not live to see it for himself.

On the potential of the arts to perform a diplomatic role, both Jacquie and Jenny express a firm belief in the viability of cultural diplomacy: "Art is able to take away all other issues. It opens up a dialogue and allows two cultures to meet informally, in a way that paves the way for a more formal connection."

Brother Joseph's work certainly testified to this. "An Invitation to Nature" brought an important ministerial party from Singapore including then-Minister of Trade and Industry, George Yeo, to Dublin, where they were met by then-Minister for Arts, Sport and Tourism, John O'Donoghue; on this occasion, a Memorandum

---

[3] As mentioned in George Yeo's speech at the official opening of "An Invitation to Nature".
[4] Corkery, Brother Vincent. *Brother Joseph McNally 1923–2002*. Ipoh: La Salle Centre, St. Michael's Institution, 2002. Print. 59.

of Understanding on Cultural Cooperation between Ireland and Singapore was signed.

. . . . .

Today, Brother Joseph's artworks, having found homes all over the world, continue to speak to the bonds forged between Ireland and Singapore. Chinese teacups are embedded in bog oak; ancient belian is shaped in Chinese characters.

From Brother Joseph's oeuvre, we pick our favourites. For Molly, it is *Poet* that she takes away from Ballintubber. In the tilt of the poet's head, his open mouth, his eyes fixed on a point in the distance, the word "vocation" resonates; the poet emerges from the bogwood in a way that is simultaneously natural and supernatural. *Vocation* — to live in service of a higher purpose, be it religious or aesthetic. Molly thinks about how she has seen this sense of calling in the members of the Ballintubber community, who are artists, musicians, priests, and educators.

Meanwhile, more than 11,000 kilometres away from home and almost lost in translation, Cheryl Julia pauses where *Woman in the Moon* is featured in the catalogue and thinks about the closing lines of that poem by Li Bai, which she learned to recite by heart in primary school: 举头望明月，低头思故乡. *I look at the moon and I think about my hometown.* This sentiment resonates in the ancient Irish bogwood from which the sculpture is cut; the Irishman in Singapore and the Singaporean girl in Ireland, and their thoughts meet in homesickness.

The authors of this article would like to express their gratitude to the McNally family and the larger Ballintubber community for being so generous with their time, for opening up their homes, and mostly for their warmth. Thanks must also go to Jacquie Moore and Jenny Deery for taking time out of their busy schedules to speak to us. This article is dedicated to the memory of Brother Joseph McNally.

. . . . .

Molly Hennigan *completed her undergraduate studies at Maynooth University majoring in English with Geography as a minor subject. She is currently at Trinity College Dublin undertaking a one year M. Phil in Irish Writing.*
Cheryl Julia Lee *is a recent English graduate from Nanyang Technological University. She is currently completing her postgraduate studies at Trinity College Dublin. Her first poetry collection,* We Were Always Eating Expired Things, *was published in 2014.*

Dr. Albert Winsemius: A Dutchman among Singapore's Pioneers

Benjamin Felix van Roij

"I have always considered that day — 9 August 1965 — as the most important day in the, however short-lived history of Singapore."[1] With these words, Dutch economist and Singapore's chief economic adviser from 1960–1984, Dr. Albert Winsemius, recognised the significance of Singapore's independence in a 1984 book that he authored.

From his first visit in October 1960 as the leader of a United Nations Development Program (UNDP) mission to advise Singapore on industrialisation, he became the city's reliable and trustful guide through difficult economic times for almost 25 years till he retired in 1984. During that time he visited Singapore two or three times a year, each time for about three weeks to review the country's economic progress, to discuss future strategy and come up with plans to transform Singapore. According to former Prime Minister Lee Kuan Yew, Singapore only paid for his plane tickets and for his hotel bills but nothing else.[2] And although he became an important advisor to the Singapore government, he was never officially appointed.[3]

A younger generation seemed less aware of the role of "the Dutchman behind Singapore Inc.", as a newspaper headline once described him. In September 1996 *The Straits Times* together with the Ministry of Education conducted a survey on post-war history among young Singaporeans. Former Prime Minister Goh Chok Tong alerted the nation that there was a "serious gap in knowledge" as the survey

---

[1] A. Winsemius, *The Dynamics of a Developing Nation: Singapore* (Singapore: Unpublished material, 1984), 11.
[2] Lee K. Y., *From Third World to First* (New York: HarperCollins, 2000), 78.
[3] S. Tan, "Dr. Albert Winsemius: Singapore's Trusted Guide," *The Straits Times*, 7 December 1996. Retrieved 4 March 2015 from http://ourstory.asia1.com.sg/dream/lifeline/win2.html.

revealed that students had little knowledge of important figures such as Dr. Albert Winsemius.[4]

Winsemius was born in 1910 in a rather small town in the Netherlands called Leeuwarden. He had worked at his father's cheese company when he was still a teenager. Finding out that working with his hands did not pay very well, he quickly discovered that he needed to go to a university to become more successful.[5] After he finished his studies at Erasmus University in Rotterdam and passed his doctoral exam in 1939, he started working for the Ministry of Economic Affairs and soon became a director-general for industrialisation in the Netherlands. After several years he left his job at the Dutch government and started working in the private sector.[6] When he left that position in 1960 he started working as an economic adviser for the United Nations. His first year as leader of an industrial survey team led him to Singapore.

Winsemius' First Visit to Singapore

One of the reasons the UNDP team came to Singapore was to recommend a certain development direction for the Asian city. The result of the United Nations Industrial Survey Mission (1960–1961) was presented in 1961 to then Prime Minister (PM) Lee Kuan Yew and became known as the Winsemius Report. An important conclusion of the Report was that the existing Industrial Promotion Board was underperforming and the Report advised that a new and stronger board — a one stop agency to attract investments — should be established.[7] The new Economic Development Board (EDB) set up in 1961 became one of the first important institutions in Singapore established to spearhead Singapore's drive towards industrialisation as a strategy for economic development.[8]

The Report also highlighted that the state had a key role in sustaining private capital, most of which would have to be attracted from overseas. The Report warned that the impending union with Malaya was no guarantee for future industrialisation. Large infrastructural development was necessary to lower the establishment and operational costs for foreign investments.[9] The Singapore government accepted and followed the recommendations of the Winsemius Report and started attracting industrial capital from overseas and invested heavily in the city's infrastructure.[10] Furthermore Winsemius recommended Singapore to create a common

---

[4] A. Koh, "Working against Globalisation: the Role of the Media and National Education in Singapore," *Globalisation, Societies and Education* 4(3) (2006), 362.
[5] S. Tan, "Dr. Albert Winsemius."
[6] E. Lee, *Singapore: The Unexpected Nation* (Singapore: ISEAS 2008), p. 269.
[7] Lee, *From Third World to First*, 77.
[8] T. J. Bellows, "Economic Challenges and Political Innovation: The Case of Singapore," *Asian Affairs* 32(4) (2006), 251.
[9] M. Hill and K. F. Lian, *The Politics of Nation Building and Citizenship in Singapore* (London: Routledge, 1995), 118.
[10] Ibid., 146–148.

market agreement with Malaysia and built a new relationship of barter trade with Indonesia. He also advised the government to seek more ways to sell Singapore-manufactured products to the markets of the US, Europe and Australia.[11]

Winsemius felt that Singapore had the key elements towards successful industrialisation. "The greatest asset is the high aptitude of her people to work in manufacturing industries. They can be ranked among the best factory workers in the world."[12] Although Winsemius was convinced Singapore would become a strong economic power in 1961 he laid down two fairly simple preconditions for the potential success: First of all, and the most important precondition, according to him was the elimination of the communists who made economic prosperity impossible. "It was obvious that the communist influence had to be eliminated, if Singapore was to come to economic development at all."[13] For Winsemius it was evident that no company would ever invest their capital in a country disordered by strikes and street riots and the communists had to be removed from government, the labour unions and from the streets. Eliminating the communists from the unions would allow the possibility of creating a new labour organisation that could contribute to the development of Singapore.[14] The second precondition was not to remove the Stamford Raffles Statue.[15] Sir Stamford Raffles was the British founder of the city of Singapore in 1819 and according to Winsemius letting the statue remain in the middle of the city would be a symbolic way of accepting the British heritage and could be used to show overseas companies the willingness of Singapore in accepting and welcoming assistance from abroad. "By letting the statue remain, I reasoned, we made it clear to foreign investors that we accepted the inheritance of the west up to the point that it would be to our advantage."[16]

"Wise and Canny"

The unexpected separation of Singapore from Malaysia just two years after the merger left Singapore in dire straits. Lee asked Dr. Winsemius to come back to Singapore and sought advice for the country's economic strategy in the wake of separation from Malaysia and losing the economic hinterland.

The government came up with a five-point plan to develop Singapore based on the recommendations from Winsemius together with the advice and work of the

---

[11] Lee, *From Third World to First*, 66.
[12] K. Tamboer, "Albert Winsemius, 'founding father' of Singapore'," *IIAS Newsletter* 9, Leiden (1996), Retrieved 4 March 2015 from http://www.iias.nl/iiasn/iiasn9/soueasia/winsemiu.html.
[13] Winsemius, *Dynamics of a Developing Nation*, 3–4.
[14] Ibid., 5.
[15] Lee, *From Third World to First*, 66–67.
[16] Winsemius, *Dynamics of a Developing Nation*, 14.

EDB and then Minister of Finance, Goh Keng Swee.[17] The first step was to set up manufacturing of low value but labour intensive industries such as the production of shirts and pyjamas. The next step was to start a housing programme (HDB) and to attract foreign enterprises. The third phase was the upgrading of the industries and actively promoting technical education. The transformation of Singapore into a new international financial centre and the creation of an international traffic and transport hub finalised the strategy.[18]

In Winsemius' oral history, he recalled wanting to transform Singapore into a financial centre for banking, with a "24-hour round-the-world service in money and banking."[19] He also mentioned the telephone call he made to his friend, the vice-president of the Bank of America in Singapore. "Look here Mr. Van Oenen, Singapore wants, within 10 years, to be the financial centre in Southeast Asia."[20] Following this phone conversation, Van Oenen wrote an article on the subject and sent it to Hon Sui Sen, then the chairman of EDB. Hon was also advised in 1968 by Winsemius to start an overseas office to create international operations.[21] And when the EDB decided to establish an overseas branch, Winsemius advised Hon that it should open its doors in New York. He even asked a Dutch retiree, who had worked for the Dutch Economic Development Board, to become its first head executive. This outward-looking strategy of the government and the EDB characterised the strength of Singapore's industrial development.[22]

Winsemius was glad to see that the government pursued an economic policy based on the capitalistic system of free trade. "I have always considered this choice to be one of the most monumental in the history of Singapore."[23] Winsemius additionally told Lee that further development of Singapore could only be obtained when the city would accept large-scale technical, managerial, entrepreneurial and marketing knowhow from Europe and the US.[24] Moreover strong ties with the West were important to get access to their booming markets and with the help of Winsemius, Dutch Royal Philips came to Singapore to establish electronics production as part of his strategy to develop high value manufacturing.[25]

---

[17] M. Hunter, "Who Rules Singapore? The Only True Mercantile State in the World," *Geopolitics, History and International Relations* 5(2) (2013), 94.
[18] Tamboer, "Albert Winsemius."
[19] Lee, *From Third World to First*, 89.
[20] Ibid., 89–90.
[21] L. H. Chua, "He Believed in Singapore's Future," *The Straits Times*, 7 December 1996. Retrieved 4 March 2015 from see: http://ourstory.asia1.com.sg/dream/lifeline/win3.html.
[22] Lee, *Singapore*, 270–271.
[23] Winsemius, *Dynamics of a Developing Nation*, 14.
[24] Lee, *From Third World to First*, 67.
[25] Hunter, "Who Rules Singapore?", 94.

Lee described Winsemius as "wise and canny" and he had learnt from him how European and American companies do business.[26] Lee's meetings with important CEOs were very productive because Winsemius told him how their minds work. During that time Winsemius' son was working at McKinsey, an American business firm, and knew very well how the Americans looked at business risks.[27] The only thing Singapore needed was to be part of that global economic system of trade and investment.

In order to keep Winsemius up to date, an EDB employee regularly sent him reports and a daily copy of *The Straits Times*. He would then come to Singapore and spend his weeks talking to government officials, company's executives and union leaders. The leaders of MNCs in Singapore soon appreciated the role Winsemius played as adviser and spoke frankly to him about the problems they faced.[28] Finally Winsemius would hand over his report with recommendations to the Minister of Finance and Lee Kuan Yew, with whom he would have a working lunch alone.[29] Lee mentioned in his memoirs that Winsemius "had a pragmatic, hands-on approach, a good head for figures, and a knack for getting grips with the basic issues, ignoring the mass of details."[30]

The Singapore Wonder

Winsemius' recommendations to focus on industrialisation and transform Singapore into a global city created the foundations for the further development of Singapore and the emergence of the high-value added high-tech industries. By the late 1960s, the communists had been eliminated, organised labour was changed into a positive element with the tripartite arrangement, and the policy of free enterprise became the basis for the fast economic development.[31]

In 1970, Winsemius advised Singapore for its next step of industrialisation. He noted that within 10 years the state-city would be fully developed and industrialised and hence it should start preparing itself in exporting brain services by investing money in new universities and technical institutes. "Except for a good harbour, Singapore has no natural resources. We shall have to earn our own living with our hands and our brains. Moreover, being a small country, we have to sell our goods and services in the world market, and be the most competitive of all. We must

---

[26] P. Ho, "Reasonable Men Adapt, Unreasonable Men Change the World," in *The Big Ideas of Lee Kuan Yew*, Chan H. C. et al. (Singapore: Straits Times Press, 2014), 93.
[27] Lee, *From Third World to First*, 74–75.
[28] Ibid., 79.
[29] Ibid., 78–79.
[30] Ibid., 79.
[31] Winsemius, *Dynamics of a Developing Nation*, 16.

therefore develop our hands and brains to their maximum: moreover keep in mind, that as a rule: brains pay better."[32]

It does seem therefore that Winsemius actually played a significant role in Singapore's success. Many of his plans were implemented and he was behind the development strategy that turned Singapore into today's high-tech and high-value-added hub.[33] Winsemius once said: "In my opinion it would be next to impossible to transplant the Singapore wonder elsewhere. It is senseless to launch an economic development program in a country which lacks political stability and does not have a government that sticks to that program in the knowledge that one day it will be recognised and rewarded by the voters."[34]

Benjamin Felix van Roij is a Master student at KU Leuven. He was an Associate at the EU Centre from September to December 2014.

---

[32] Ibid., 21.
[33] Chua, "He Believed in Singapore's Future."
[34] Tamboer, "Albert Winsemius."

The Polish Professor Who "Maps our Brains" — Prof. Dr. Wieslaw L. Nowiński

Charles Chia

In the first few decades of independence, few would have envisioned Singapore on the cutting edge of scientific research and development as it is now. With many large multinational companies (MNCs) already established in Singapore, the government began shifting its focus to more capital- and knowledge-intensive fields. This saw the creation of the National Science and Technology Board (NSTB) which was operationalised under the Ministry of Trade and Industry on 11 January 1991, and 11 years later it was renamed as the Agency for Science, Technology and Research (A*STAR).

Through the years, a diverse and ever-increasing pool of international scientists and researchers has worked for and with A*STAR; some were recruited in the most recent decade while others have been around since its early beginnings. Professor Dr. Wieslaw L. Nowiński came to Singapore in 1991 for an initial one year, but admitted that an excellent organisation led him to stay for 23. He liked and admired the clear vision, solid strategy and supportive R&D environment which the Singapore government provided and decided to stay.

As Director and Principal Scientist of the Biomedical Imaging Lab in the Singapore Biomedical Imaging Consortium (SBIC), Dr. Nowiński has been involved in a whole range of activities. This included research, generating Intellectual Property (IP), publishing papers, pursuing local and international collaboration, developing products for commercialisation, starting high-tech spinoffs and managing a team and training students. Dr. Nowinski has served in roles ranging from Research Associate to Adjunct Professor at Nanyang Technological University.

The distinguished scientist was most recently nominated as a Finalist for the 2014 European Inventor Award under the Lifetime Achievement Category granted by the European Patent Office (EPO). The EPO noted that Dr. Nowiński had "developed 34 different brain atlases that are used for research and education, as well as for the diagnosis, prediction and treatment of brain disorders such as Parkinson's, stroke and psychiatric conditions", and in that way, he had truly "revolutionised the world of brain mapping". In 2013, he was awarded the Pioneer in Medicine Award by the Society for Brain Mapping and Therapeutics in the United States. Back home, Dr. Nowiński was a recipient of the Outstanding Pole Award 2012 by the Polish Foundation Poland Now. It highlights and honours outstanding personalities who are well known and respected abroad but may not be as well recognised in Poland.

During his time spent at the Lab, Dr. Nowiński witnessed first-hand the multitude of organisational changes and the incredible growth of A*STAR. The figures that tell his story are indeed remarkable. His efforts over the years have resulted in more than 500 publications, 51 patents filed (32 granted), 42 awards, 35 brain atlas products licensed to 63 companies and institutions worldwide, and three spinoff companies which he does not manage.

Dr. Nowiński previously spent two years organising the Institute of Bioengineering (now the Institute of Bioengineering and Nanotechnology) while contributing to extensive collaboration with international and local institutions. He received the NUS Outstanding University Researcher Award in 1998 during his time with Kent Ridge Digital Labs. He has worked with a significant number of distinguished international and local institutions, including Singapore's National Neuroscience Institute, National Cancer Centre, National University Hospital, Tan Tock Seng Hospital, Singapore General Hospital and the Singapore Eye Research Institute. His international collaborations include the Johns Hopkins Hospital, Mayo Clinic, Philips Research, ETH Zürich and the Montreal Neurological Institute. His efforts have not gone unnoticed by the media either, with outlets from *The Wall Street Journal* to the Discovery Channel featuring his work. It is safe to say that in his field, Dr. Nowiński has successfully put Singapore on the global map. The abundance of projects that he has wholeheartedly led and poured all of his time into is a testament of Dr. Nowiński's desire to help Singapore build its dreams of being a knowledgeable and prosperous nation. The President of the European Patent Office, Mr. Benoit Battistelli, added that Dr. Nowiński's work "brings research and practice together and as a European world citizen, he builds bridges between continents".

Beyond his scientific endeavours, Dr. Nowiński has helped to foster relations between Poland and Singapore. There are approximately 800 Poles in Singapore today. He participated in recruitment trips to attract Polish students and scientists to Singapore and chaired a delegation from A*STAR, NUS and NTU which covered some 2,000 kilometres across Poland.

Scientific links between the two countries have grown in part due to his efforts. A*STAR and the Polish Ministry of Science and Higher Education (MSHE) signed a Memorandum of Understanding (MoU) in January 2005 and renewed it in February 2011. Dr. Nowiński even personally spoke to Donald Tusk, then Polish Prime Minister (and from December 2014 President of the European Council) when he visited Singapore in late 2012. The MoU provides a platform for R&D collaboration and knowledge exchange.

Dr. Nowiński describes Poland and Singapore as fulfilling a similar role in being a bridge between the East and the West despite their geographical distance. Soon after his arrival in Singapore, Dr. Nowiński wrote a letter to the then President of Poland Lech Wałęsa encouraging the fostering of relations between the two countries. Having received the Outstanding Pole Award afforded him some media reach to promote Polish-Singapore relations.

Dr. Nowiński's family has also contributed to art in Singapore. When you travel downtown on the East Coast Parkway, near Keppel on the left side in CHIJ Kellock Primary School is a beautiful and colourful five-storey stained glass window designed by his wife. The plaque below the stained glass window says: "*The original full-scale design with details and glass arrangement were done by Dr. Anna Halina Nowinska of Poland. She donated this piece of her one-year work to the school where her two daughters found their second home.*" Two more stained glass windows designed by Dr. Anna Nowińska decorate public places in Singapore. The *Dragonfly* metal sculpture in Gardens by the Bay is a symbol of the world's peace and the Nowiński family has had ongoing discussions with its local creator to have a copy of this symbol also in Warsaw.

What Dr. Nowiński first noticed when he came to Singapore was its friendly, thoughtful, and warm environment. He laments that in recent years, the pace of change has been increasingly drastic, particularly in public places and the Mass Rapid Transit system. He acknowledges that R&D strategy has been excellent but notes that execution could be improved at the lower levels, mostly due to a high manpower turnover within A*STAR. Dr. Nowiński adds that a greater emphasis on technology validation would facilitate its R&D commercialisation.

Singapore has done a great job in the area of organising joint scientific workshops, inviting scientists and supporting student exchanges. However, Dr. Nowiński suggests that decision-makers and policymakers should not limit such research exchanges to a select few countries as the EU has 28 member countries with a tremendous pool of talent and boundless opportunities for collaboration.

After 23 years in Singapore, Dr. Nowiński's lab was closed in December 2014 and he will be leaving Singapore for the US. However, we hope that Singapore's connections with Dr. Nowiński and his home country, Poland will continue and be strengthened in other ways.

References

A*STAR. (2012). A*STAR 20th Anniversary Commemorative Publication. Retrieved 4 March 2015 from http://www.a-star.edu.sg/About-A-STAR/20th-Anniversary-Commemorative-Publication.aspx.

Dr. Wieslaw Nowinski — Creator of the "World's Most Gorgeous" Human Brain Atlases. (n.d.). EURAXESS Researchers in Motion. Retrieved 4 March 2015 from http://ec.europa.eu/euraxess/index.cfm/links/meet_the_researcher/asean.

Nowiński, W. L. (n.d.). Personal Website. Retrieved 4 March 2015 from http://www.wieslawNowiński.com/.

"Outstanding Pole Award." Teraz Polska (2012) [in Polish]. Retrieved 4 March 2015 from http://www.terazpolska.pl/pl/Laureaci-III-edycji.

Prime Minister's Visit to Asia: Poland–Singapore Commercial Relations. (2012, November 3). Retrieved 4 March 2015 from https://www.premier.gov.pl/en/news/news/prime-ministers-visit-to-asia-poland-singapore-commercial-relations.html.

Prof. Nowiński: Brain Research Might Become a Polish Specialty (2013, August 23). *Polish Press Agency*. Retrieved 4 March 2015 from http://www.naukawpolsce.pap.pl/en/news/news,396779,prof-Nowiński-brain-research-might-become-a-polish-specialty.html.

Singapore-based Brain Research Specialist Wieslaw L. Nowiński Nominated for the European Inventor Award. (2014, April 29). *PRNewswire*. Retrieved 4 March 2015 from http://finance.yahoo.com/news/singapore-based-brain-research-specialist-080000646.html.

Singapore Bioimaging Consortium. (n.d.). Collaborations. Retrieved 4 March 2015 from https://www.a-star.edu.sg/sbic/RESEARCH/Academic-Groups-Units/Biomedical-Imaging-Lab/Collaborations.aspx.

Singapore Bioimaging Consortium. (n.d.). Research Academic Groups. Retrieved 4 March 2015 from https://www.a-star.edu.sg/sbic/RESEARCH/Academic-Groups-Units.aspx.

Tan, S. (2013, November 1). Straits Times: Singapore, Poland Pledge to Bolster Links. *Straits Times*. Retrieved 4 March 2015 from http://www.mfa.gov.sg/content/mfa/media_centre/singapore_headlines/2013/201310/news_20131101.html.

Charles Chia was a research intern in the EU Centre in Singapore from September 2014 to February 2015. He graduated with a Bachelor of Journalism after studying in Melbourne and Utrecht. Charles now works in a risk management consultancy in the security and investigations industry.

Art and Science in Singapore in the Last 15 Years — A Personal Journey and Reflection

Isabelle Desjeux

When I arrived in Singapore, in 1999, it was to take up a job in one of the newest Life Science Institutes located on the NUS Campus. Both my husband (a Malaysian) and myself (a French citizen) are biologists, and these offers to work here were to be an opportunity for myself to discover Asia and for my husband to be close to his family (living in Kuala Lumpur) for a while.

As a scientist, I have always considered myself a citizen of the world. I studied in France, then in Scotland, and worked in Germany. During my time in the lab, I spent a substantial amount of time in England and in the US. So, I thought spending two years in a multicultural lab in Singapore would be the same. Being part of a field of research is like being part of a large multinational and multicultural family. Each lab will generally have people from different countries; you read articles relating to your field written by people of many different nationalities, and you chat with colleagues from around the world who are the only other people who might know as well as you the role of such molecule or the biological mechanism you are so interested in. I was not disappointed. As I started working in Dr. Mohan Subramaniam's lab at the then named Institute of Molecular Agrobiology (or IMA), I met Singaporeans, Indians, Scots, French, Germans, Dutch, Chinese, and so on in my lab, and other neighbouring labs. And sure enough, there was no culture shock, as we had read the same articles and used the same protocols, attended the same conferences. It was also a great experience to work in a brand new institute where the sky seemed to be the limit for what material would be put at the scientists' disposal.

As life has it though, I was at a crossroads, and having arrived in Singapore with two very young daughters, I soon found that spending so much of my time away from them to work in the lab was not a satisfying way to bring them up. I also found myself too distracted in the lab to be as efficient as I would have liked. I was also doing more and more art, and found that my time was stretched between these different commitments. I therefore resolved to leave the lab to focus on my second carrier as an artist, hoping that it would also allow me to spend more time with my daughters.

Much of the early years were spent painting and making art from home. But I also took night classes at the Nanyang Academy of Fine Arts (NAFA) and I would say this was my first venture into meeting and bonding with Singaporeans. I walked out of my comfort zone, and was delighted to meet young and old people committed to doing art after long hours at work (for most of them). However, I found a strong disconnect between my learning to paint and what I thought I wanted to make art for; I also struggled to connect with fellow students as it seems we were after different goals. I enjoyed the craft of painting and print-making that I was learning, as well as *papier mâché*, that I was doing from home but I found that none of this was helping me express how I saw the world around me, with all its quirkiness and absurdity. In these early days, I also received many disapproving comments from people wondering how one could jump from science into art, two such disconnected subjects. What people seemed to object to mostly was the idea that I was "wasting" the years I had spent educating myself in science now that I was "only painting".

I personally never understood it as a waste since I grew up to see education as a means to learn how to think and gain experience in general. This experience can be applied in a variety of domains. And one of the things I have learnt from working in a lab is that the wider the peoples' background, the more dynamic the team is. This means not only people of various nationalities, but also from a variety of technical backgrounds. For example, a team including a microbiologist, a chemist, a physiologist and a cell biologist is more likely to solve an unusual problem than a team comprising only cell biologists, because people have to learn to speak without jargon, and there is no silly question, since everyone is outside a field. It means that being an outsider is an asset, and being a scientist in a world of artists will bring new ways of looking at things and, similarly for an artist in a lab. This might also explain why multinational labs fare better.

Eventually, I returned to the lab as an artist. In the UK, there would have been a way to apply for funding for such a position (The Wellcome Trust has been funding Artists-in-Labs since the mid-1990s, and has set the trend for artists-in-labs in the UK), but in Singapore at the time, this was just done in a non-official way. I was artist-in-residence in Dr. Oliferenko's lab at Temasek Life Sciences Laboratory (TLL), as IMA had become known. Officially, I was also the designer for the yearly symposium poster, which meant that I spent time understanding the kind of research going on in the labs. I was using some of the equipment in the lab, and watching people interact and work. And I got interested in telling the story of what is happening in the lab. This eventually became a series of artworks; the project was called "Story Sculptures", and consisted of talking to scientists whose lab had recently published a paper. I collected all their drafts (from the recycling bin) and produced small paper sculptures that I gifted back to the scientist, giving them the name of the article it came from. It was meant to represent the article they had just written and remind them of the trial and error that was required before the story came out as a "paper" (article). Often when an article is published, all the earlier drafts do not seem to matter anymore and can be forgotten, leading to a bias in our memory. Hence the sculptures were meant as a reminder of the process and hard work that resulted in the final act — the published paper. The project didn't attract much attention outside the lab, despite being part of a solo exhibition I held in 2007. People were still not used to the idea of collaborations between scientists and artists.

A few months after the "Story Sculptures" solo exhibition came a breakthrough. During those years as an artist-in-residence, I had been designing yearly posters for TLL's symposiums. This involved imagining some of the scientific findings as illustrations for posters. Eventually, a scientist friend who knew my work gave my name to Swissnex, which was looking for a second artist to exhibit alongside Ariel Ruiz y Altaba's show "Minimal Landscapes". Although my art didn't get shown, I did attend the opening of the exhibition and had a chance encounter with Dr. Ian Woo, who was at the time running the postgraduate program at Lasalle College of Arts. He convinced me to apply for the Masters in Fine Arts program, and I did. This was a great experience in learning a more formal way of thinking about my art, talking about it, and researching. It led me to finally meet with some of the most interesting artists in the region and beyond, as local artists and artists travelling through Singapore would often stop and give talks in Lasalle. I also met among the students the most interesting mixture of people, both Singaporean and foreigners, and people from all walks of life, from a shipbuilder to a mathematician, a bartender, a theatre practitioner, a lecturer in English, and a designer. What I found most exciting was to be able to build a common culture during the 18 months we spent together in the Masters' studio at Lasalle, each working on a different project, but each influencing each other, in the way all interdisciplinary projects can. By this time, people in Singapore seemed blasé about the possibility of a scientist being an artist: "It's all the same thing, isn't it?" I now heard people saying, a bit optimistically, "How things have changed in 10 years!" Truthfully, many of my artworks wouldn't have existed if I hadn't been able to collaborate closely with a Russell Morton, a then student of the Puttnam School of Film, located one floor below the Masters' Studio. In 2012, after winning the French-Singapore New Generation artist (an initiative from the Société Générale Banking Gallerie at the Alliance

Française), I spent a couple of weeks in a lab in Cambridge (UK) and presented the work done in the lab in a solo exhibition back in Singapore, highlighting the importance of risk-taking (and therefore the high occurrence of failures) to make ground-breaking discoveries.

I started life as an artist 15 years ago. I graduated from Lasalle five years ago, all this while in Singapore. In the last five years, Art and Science has become a possibility in Singapore, as the city aims to become a renaissance city. New groups have emerged here, from Biohackers to DIY-Bio groups involving ordinary citizens learning to run simple experiments in their kitchen and change the world around them, or groups getting artists and scientists to work together, or the newest Open Call by the Substation, calling for an "Art and Science Project", and the ArtScience Museum actually providing insights into interdisciplinary works, from exhibitions to performance and providing a platform for young designers out to change the world with new inventions. Singapore can even boast of its own pool of Art-Scientists on the international scale, from photographer Robert Zhao Renhui to musician Bani Haykal and various New Media artists. In 2009, Singapore even hosted the ISEA (Inter-Society for Electronic Arts), and there has been an artist-in-residents' initiative at NUS since 2011.

New international events such as the Singapore Night Festival, or the i Light Marina Bay festival of lights have been attracting new media artists from Singapore and around the world to produce a different kind of public art; art fairs have multiplied in recent years too, although these currently still stick to traditional media of painting, drawing, print and sculpture. Schools are now calling artists to support science teachers to help students understand concepts better. The maker movement is blurring the line between designers, engineers, artists, crafters. Truly, there is no better time to be an art-scientist in Singapore!

What I see as an artist and a scientist having been trained to understand the two different cultures, is a thirst to break down the boundaries and embrace differences, opening the door to new ways of making art, creating and using knowledge in Singapore.

Dr. Isabelle Desjeux is an independent artist and Creative Director at Playeum (Play Museum).

Beppe De Vito — The Italian Restaurateur

Charles Chia

&Sons was gearing up for the lunchtime crowd as I strolled in one late morning for a chat with its owner Mr. Beppe De Vito. The Singapore Permanent Resident is probably a household name for those familiar with the restaurant scene in Singapore, especially for those with a penchant for authentic Italian cuisine. The list of restaurants he has worked with or is currently managing is distinctively well recognised in the local scene: these include Bice, Forlino, Garibaldi, ilLido, Latteria Mozzarella Bar and his latest venture, &Sons. Mr. De Vito would have spent two decades in Singapore in 2015 and the EU Centre felt it was apt to pick apart the thoughts of an Italian who has lived here longer than in his hometown.

The Early Years

Mr. De Vito left Italy at the tender age of 17, spending five years in London and Paris before he was sent to Singapore by the renowned Bice Group to open an outlet at Goodwood Park Hotel in 1995. In less than a year, he was largely trusted to independently manage the place as his supervisor only visited once every quarter. At 24, this was the perfect opportunity for him to gain some management experience at a restaurant which raked in S$6 million annually, considered a massive production during the 1990s and the first of its kind. There existed only a handful of other Italian restaurants at that time, namely Da Paolo, Pasta Fresca Da Salvatore, Domvs, Fratini La Trattoria and the now-defunct Ristorante Bologna. Mr. De Vito was due to head back to Europe for a management course but decided he wanted to open something to call his own. His plans did not work out since it was difficult to convince investors that a 20-something could open a restaurant and compete with established names in the scene.

Mr. De Vito then did stints at the Marina Mandarin, Singapore and in Hong Kong as a means to gain investors' confidence in his maturity. He returned from Hong Kong to Singapore thereafter and the rest, as the cliché goes, is history. Looking back, he points to the manner in which Singapore bounced back from the 1997 Asian financial crisis as giving him confidence in the future of the country; further, he was amazed at the rapid pace of change and was excited to be in the thick of the action as Singapore sped into the 21st century. He had already spent five years in Singapore by the time he returned and felt comfortable in the local scene.

Recounting the opening of his flagship restaurant ilLido in 2006, Mr. De Vito admitted that people thought he was crazy to choose Sentosa, especially since the island was significantly different back then. Mr. De Vito, however, saw opportunity in the space and invested what the place deserved, which he felt was the only way to attract people all the way out there. He later did the same with Forlino — a further step up for clientele that wanted an even more luxurious and exclusive experience than that of ilLido. Mr. De Vito noted that the three Ls (location, location, location) began applying to tiny Singapore after MBS opened and made the Marina Bay area a focal point. Two months after launching Forlino in 2008, the global financial crisis hit and Mr. De Vito had to adapt swiftly in terms of operation cost and pricing, eventually turning it back to success and later selling it.

Reflecting on the changes in the local dining scene, Mr. De Vito said that it used to be a less sophisticated environment where restaurants were opened on the cheap and true quality was notably absent. He highlighted the role of statutory boards SPRING Singapore (Standards, Productivity and Innovation Board) and the Economic Development Board (EDB) in helping local companies evolve through marketing and branding themselves more deftly, quoting the example of home-grown Crystal Jade Culinary Concept Holdings expanding across Asia and most recently opening its first restaurant in San Francisco.

Above all, Mr. De Vito credited one unmistakable catalyst behind the most recent burgeoning of the dining scene — the 2010 opening of Marina Bay Sands (MBS) and Resorts World Sentosa. MBS alone altered not only the urban landscape with its unique architecture but also the culinary landscape; celebrity chefs were lured here and dining standards and expectations rose in tandem. The average person outside Singapore generally did not know much about this country until the casinos opened. More professionals, including chefs who had perfected their craft in Michelin-starred restaurants, were arriving and this meant more competition in the field which created a buzz and impacted the local dining scene. In many instances, Singapore also has better access to fresh regional ingredients than Europe, fostering a creative fusion of flavours in kitchens across the city-state.

Mr. De Vito predicted that this trend towards more innovative and diverse dining will continue moving forward, that what is the minority today — top-end, well-executed and well-planned restaurants — will become bigger and bigger as more and more professionals are brought in. He referred to a good sample of local chefs who have spun-off and done great things, not just Justin Quek, Andre Chiang and Iggy but many other younger Singaporeans who have opened bakeries, cafes and casual places that have added vibrancy to the local scene.

The Evolving Dining Scene in Singapore — Better Service, Mutual Respect

Singapore has increasingly been compared to global cities like London and Paris, but Mr. De Vito contends that the little red dot has not been able to catch up in terms of the attitudes of customers and service staff. Europe is understandably ahead culturally as they have had a much longer history in terms of fine dining while Singapore has really only had such European-styled establishments in the last two to three decades. The higher pace of growth and affluence here, however, bodes well for Singapore in catching up with its European counterparts. Mr. De Vito observed that guests here are not as appreciative of what is being done and forget that professionals are behind the presented plate. He stressed that respect for the craft was missing, and that there were high expectations without an understanding of the reality.

Moreover, Mr. De Vito recognised that there was still a stigma attached to chefs and the public perception that it was a lowly career choice. He explained that little existed between the two extremes of celebrity chefs and the average cooks, lamenting that there were chefs who knew they were good but behaved like prima donnas and expected to jump from the bottom to the top in an instant without understanding that it took a lot more to succeed. In Europe, there is a widespread acceptance that if the worker does his job well he will naturally get promoted as people take notice. On the other hand, customer expectations rule the day in Singapore and maturity and confidence in customer-staff interaction are still absent. Additionally, he felt that there is still a certain lack of respect for workmanship and for service staff. While the quality of the food and design are now on par with restaurants in cities like London, Paris, Rome or New York, the culture of service and respect is lacking. Mr. De Vito suggested that Singapore still needed some time to grow. "Anyone can have a good and bad day but everyone deserves a chance. Sometimes high expectations by customers often turn to impatience."

Mr. De Vito believes that as a society, Singapore is still young, and inexperienced, noting the tendency of pointing a finger at someone whenever something happens.

"Singapore is a big city and people need to understand that is who we are. I think Singapore would grow much faster culturally if we begin to understand that we are city-dwellers in a metropolis. We are at the heart of evolution; everything has grown through metropolises, through Paris, London, New York. Nothing happens through small kampongs or towns in the world. Singapore has so much good going on that the little annoyances and irritations appearing every day lower the whole experience. Everybody is ready to complain but nobody is willing to do anything to improve the situation."

By and large, however, Mr. De Vito proudly affirms that he would rather be in Singapore than anywhere else in the world. While acknowledging that there was a segment of expatriate Caucasians that enjoyed feeling different, like they do not belong here and are the big fish in the small pond, he asserted that he feels very local. Mr. De Vito is married to a Singaporean Chinese and has four Singaporean kids, including one from a previous marriage to a Singaporean Chinese as well. He is equally proud of eating more local than Italian food. In a profile on CNN Travel, Mr. De Vito remarked that he enrolled his children in local rather than international schools, that they will eventually have to do National Service, and that this was where his family felt most at home.

Food and the Future

The arts and cultural scene has seen a burst of productions local and international while a diverse mix of new galleries, theatres and museums is regularly opened. More Singaporeans have now travelled and lived in other global cities of culture and brought back with them a myriad of habits and tastes. Mr. De Vito cites the coffee scene as the embodiment of this continuing trend, "If you wanted a good espresso five years ago you had to go to an Italian restaurant. Independent roasters are now booming and not radically different to Melbourne or San Francisco."

Good food is of course much more than simple pleasure or fuel for the body. The restaurateur has always believed in food (Italian, no less) being a bridge between cultures.

"You can meet somebody from a different culture and not share the language but the food will unite and be the common thing during that meal. I've seen that. I've been lucky enough to have been here such a long time. Even when I was in Europe, playing host to meetings of all sorts; official, unofficial, business, friendly, neighbours catching up for the first time, bankers entertaining locals and vice versa, politicians, presidents, actors, with many different cultures and by the end of the meal, nothing was different, they were all the same. So if there's one thing that definitely can unite people anywhere in the world, it's the food."

Mr. De Vito exuded a genuine desire to be seen as local, but admitted that people here were instinctively classifying him as a foreigner based on his looks alone on a daily basis. He added, "I know it's the consequence of certain people enjoying their privilege, feeling special and different."

Pondering the next 50 years, Mr. De Vito hoped for his children to have it as good as it is now, that they could also experience a more mature and self-assured Singapore and not be afraid of being small, nor of not saying or doing the right thing.

"It should become more innate as we go on, the appreciation for the little things, the respect for everyone and the aim to do better and better each time. It's still pretty much money-driven now. I hope that people do get to accept themselves more and not feel frustrated about not being able to afford the 5Cs or whatever it is. Singapore has always been learning for the past 50 years from other places in every industry and we all know that … I hope we can now learn from the best societies without looking too far. Singapore has everything going for it to be a New York, where you got multi-layered society in every aspect, more languages spoken there than anywhere else in the world and yet it works really well. It is important that we all learn how to treat each other better, to have more respect and allow people to make mistakes as opposed to the fear of people who may make mistakes. We have 50 years of having gone from zero to hero in terms of number, let's now grow culturally."

He emphasised that this change had to begin from parents and grandparents — that acceptance of diversity should be paramount. Ultimately, he confessed that he respected efficiency and Singapore is the epitome of that which he valued.

"Every policy will upset somebody; it's about making the majority happy. If I want to do it, I can do it no matter who I am because the system will help me."

Mr. De Vito conceded that with four kids and multiple businesses on his hands, he had become increasingly busy over the years and was unable to get more involved with the Italian community as opposed to when he first arrived. He noticed that most European expatriates came with their families when he first arrived but that there were more young singles and couples now. There is now a more diverse cross-section of professionals who are based here, and young adults who are here for one to two years. There is a similar diversity in the industries in which Italian firms have made a presence, including legal firms and consultancies, as well as manufacturers. Mr. De Vito has recently been getting back into the scene (of the Italian community) though, as he catered for the Italian embassy for their year-end dinner last year (2014). He still travels to Italy for two weeks a year and spoke appreciatively of its natural and architectural beauty.

"Italy's diversity of geography, its natural beauty and quality craftsmanship are remarkable. It makes you wonder why they are not doing better, there's a breakdown in society. As a place to visit, Venice, Rome, the whole country is an open-air museum, I'm proud to bring my kids there now and then. Europe is a beautiful place to go back to."

But when asked if Singapore was home, he replied:

"Absolutely, it's my home. I feel more Singaporean than Italian perhaps."

References

Interview with Mr. Beppe De Vito.

Chan, A. (2011, August 8). 5 Reasons Why Expats Love Singapore. *CNN*. Retrieved 4 March 2015 from http://travel.cnn.com/singapore/life/five-reasons-why-expats-love-singapore-550132.

Charles Chia was a research intern in the EU Centre in Singapore from September 2014 to February 2015. He graduated with a Bachelor of Journalism after studying in Melbourne and Utrecht. Charles now works in a risk management consultancy in the security and investigations industry.

From Croatia to Singapore: Marko Kraljević's Journey

Dexter Lee

Another chapter in Singapore sports history was made on 7 November 2014, when S-League club Balestier Khalsa clinched its first Singapore Cup title after defeating heavyweights Home United Football Club at the Jalan Besar Stadium by a score of 3–1.[1] Certainly, Balestier's victory was memorable when one considers the club's trophy-less history in the S-League prior to 2013, but it was also a sweet one as it was delivered by a man who has had a two-decade long association with the club and had only picked up the role of head coach — his first senior coaching role in his entire career — just 10 months earlier. Two days after the final, the "rookie" by the name of Marko Kraljević was named S-League Coach of the Year[2] — the highest personal accolade that a football coach can receive in Singapore.

Marko Kraljević is certainly not the first European to contribute to the development of professional football in Singapore — players such as Jorg Steinebrunner, Daniel Bennett and Aleksandar Đurić have lit up the S-League and have achieved plenty. In the 2014 season the S-League had a total of 20 Europeans who have contributed to the S-League in different capacities. Meanwhile, European coaches have had great success with S-League clubs here — the likes of Alex Weaver and Patrick Vallée spring to mind. For some, success has gone beyond the S-League: long term residents Bennett and Đurić eventually decided to become Singapore citizens in order to play for the Singapore national football team, while others have moved onto greener pastures after their formative stint here — the former Sengkang Marine forward Grant Holt, who went on to play for such teams as Aston Villa

---

[1] J. H. Phoon, "Historic Cup Victory for Tigers," *VOXSPORTS*, 8 November 2014. Retrieved 4 March 2015 from http://voxsports.co/historic-cup-victory-for-tigers.
[2] S. Abdul Aziz, "S. League Awards: Rookie Kraljevic is Coach of the Year," *AsiaOne*, 12 November 2014. Retrieved 4 March 2015 from http://news.asiaone.com/news/sports/s-league-awards-rookie-kraljevic-coach-year.

and Norwich City, and currently (December 2014) plays for Huddersfield Town, is one such player.

Marko Kraljević's journey in Singapore football is certainly unique. Although the Croat and Singapore Permanent Resident (PR) is not as decorated as some of the illustrious players mentioned above, he has played for nearly a decade in Singapore and contributed to the initial development of the S-League. Even after his retirement from playing football, he has worked towards becoming a successful football coach, and in the process of doing so, he has also helped many young Singapore footballers in their careers. Last but not least, Marko Kraljević has also taken a bold step forward by becoming a successful entrepreneur in the business of futsal. His long association with Singapore, together with a list of humble contributions that has had a positive impact on Singapore's football development, is a unique story that deserves to be told.

Living the S-League Dream

Marko Kraljević has had football in his blood as long as he can remember. Growing up as a child in his hometown Osijek, he played football with his friends on the streets which helped to develop his physical, creative and mental skills. These experiences would serve him well in the later years of his life as a player, and shape how Kraljević approaches the game in Singapore today. At the time when he was growing up, young children in Croatia dreamt of playing football at European giants such as AC Milan and Bayern Munich. "For us in Eastern Europe, football is everything. And if there's an opportunity to go abroad, take it!" he tells us. As a teenager, Kraljević achieved his dream of becoming a footballer when he signed up for the main club in his hometown NK Osijek, thereby following the footsteps of Davor Šuker and Robert Špehar, who had also played for Osijek and later the Croatian national team.

The dream move to play abroad came to fruition in 1991, but rather than Western Europe, it was to a different part of the world. Malaysia's Kelantan FA made a successful bid for him, ironically beating back an approach by Singapore's Malaysia League team in the process. The settling-in process in Kelantan was smooth due to the presence of players and coaches from Croatia, and the hardworking young Croat quickly won the hearts of Kelantan fans with his footballing ability. At the same time, Kraljević also began to develop a close connection with Singapore — during the Malaysian season breaks, he would turn out alongside fellow Croatian Goran Paulic to play for Balestier United[3] — a club that he would soon have a long history with — in the Singapore Premier League.[4]

---

[3] Balestier Khalsa has had several name changes over the years. Originally founded on 10 October 1898 as Fathul Karib Football Club, the club was renamed Balestier United Recreation Club in 1975 and played in the Singapore Premier League until 1995. It changed its name to Balestier Central in 1996 before the club's entry into the S-League, and later merged with Clementi Khalsa to form Balestier Khalsa.

[4] The Singapore Premier League was the predecessor of today's S-League.

Kraljević's full-time foray into Singapore began when the Singapore League (S-League) was founded after the Football Association of Singapore (FAS) withdrew the Singapore Lions from Malaysian football competitions in 1995 due to a dispute over gate receipts.[5] Singapore's shock exit quickly gave way to excitement when the inaugural eight-team S-League geared up for an April 1996 launch. At this time, Kraljević was winning trophies with Hong Kong's Rangers FC but he was persuaded by Balestier's management to return to Singapore in March 1996. "It was not bad playing in Hong Kong but I was more familiar with Singapore." His return to Singapore coincided with the arrival of exciting new European players such as Croatia's Goran Paulic and Jure Ereš — in fact, the S-League that year started out with 17 Europeans where Croatian players made up the largest group.

Although his S-League playing career was ultimately trophy-less, Kraljević had six good seasons in the S-League with three different S-League clubs — in particular his partnership with Goran Paulic and the Yugoslav duo of Ljutvo Bogućanin and Esad Sejdic in 1996 was one that served Balestier Central well. The quartet helped Balestier to well-deserved third place S-League finishes that year, and in the 1997 and 1998 seasons, the trio of Paulic, Sedjic and Kraljević helped the club to further top-half finishes. Kraljević later moved on together with Sejdic to Tampines Rovers in 1998 before ending his S-League career with Singapore legend V. Sundramoothy's Jurong FC in 2001.

In terms of his most memorable moment as an S-League player, Kraljević counts the S-League All-Stars game against English Premier League club Newcastle United in August 1996. The match involved the best players that Singapore football had to feature in 1996, and their opponents were arguably one of the best teams in the world — if not England — at the time. Indeed, Newcastle's exciting squad boasted the likes of Les Ferdinand, David Ginola and Faustino Asprilla, and were managed by Newcastle and Liverpool legend Kevin Keegan. As Kraljević fondly recalled, "It was amazing to play to a full house against Newcastle and as a soccer player, you love this atmosphere." That game finished 5–0 to the Geordies but for Kraljević, it was clearly a moment that he has cherished for a long time.

As observed by the notable columnist Neil Humphreys, the S-League during Kraljević's playing days was a "Mustafa Shopping Centre of football players"[6] — the league had some of the best European talents, as well as non-European internationals such as 1998 Iranian World Cup stars Majid Namjoo-Motlagh and Alireza Mansourian. Indeed, Kraljević noted that back then the S-League was one

---

[5] The Singapore Lions team had won the Malaysian (Malayan) Cup 24 times — at the time of Singapore exit, the Lions' track record was second only to the Malaysian state side of Selangor. The Football Association of Singapore would re-enter the Malaysian league in 2012 with the Lions XII.

[6] N. Humphreys, "The S. League is Clearly Dying, But Who Really Cares?" *FourFourTwo*, 6 November 2014. Retrieved 4 March 2015 from http://www.fourfourtwo.com/sg/features/sleague-clearly-dying-who-really-cares.

of the best leagues he had played in, but by the time he hung up his boots, the Eastern European and Middle Eastern talent pools available to S-League clubs had begun to dry up. These were circumstances beyond the league's control, he surmises, as fewer players from Eastern Europe were available for hire due to the resurgence of professional leagues in the Balkans and the Middle East. Nevertheless, with the playing years of his career behind Kraljević, the next stage in life in Singapore would involve his taking a crack at being a successful coach, even if it meant starting from scratch.

Dreams, Hard Work and Discipline

Picking up the basics was something Kraljević felt that he needed to do when he embarked on his coaching career. "As [Jose] Mourinho once said, you have to go step by step and not jump straight into first-team management," quips Kraljević. Like the world famous Portuguese manager, the Croat started off as a youth coach — he continued with Jurong FC as a coach with the club's Centre of Excellence (COE) before returning to Balestier to manage its youth setup. During his decade long coaching career, Kraljević also earned himself a UEFA "A" Coaching License. Looking back, Kraljević felt that the youth coaching experience was a good one. "At that time I learned a lot by putting a line-up and adapting my tactics after a defeat, step by step." This approach to learning eventually opened the door to many opportunities for Kraljević, who masterminded a successful coaching stint with the Singapore Institute of Management (SIM) football team, the Balestier and Woodlands Prime League (Under-23) teams, as well the Balestier Khalsa S-League team in 2014.

However, coaching young players in Singapore did present Kraljević with some challenges along the way. "It was a shock for U-16 and U-18 players who came for trials and discovered that they had to undergo a European style training and playing regime," he remembers. Many 16-year-olds were eventually dissuaded by their parents from taking up football due to the tough training regime. Also, Kraljević recognised that most Singaporeans have a strong interest in football for social rather than professional reasons. "People love the game here and I can see many people playing in the Cosmo (Amateur) League on the weekends," he says, but many young and talented adults — especially those whom he coached at SIM — eventually gave up the game because they cannot commit to playing football as a full-time career. As he notes, this phenomenon of football as a social activity is something that does not exist in Croatia and even perhaps more widely in Europe where schoolchildren and teenagers hone their skills from a very young age with an aim to make it as professionals.

Nevertheless, for the teenagers who are fortunate enough to have jumped these hurdles to pursue a long-term football career, Kraljević has two key philosophies he learnt in Croatia that he shares with them. "Players here must dream big — they must have a dream to play for the big clubs abroad and not just be satisfied to play for Home United or Warriors FC." Here, he cited the example of Croatia where young children are constantly looking to emulate national stars such as Luka Modrić and Mario Mandžukić who are now playing in Spain's La Liga. Discipline and hard work are traits that Singaporeans are familiar with, but for Kraljević, these are even more important in the sporting field. "In Croatia, we don't see situations where players give an excuse that they're not feeling well and can't play." In Kraljević's book, aspiring professionals cannot live off excuses — they need to work hard and learn for themselves if they want to succeed in a competitive sport environment, be it at home or abroad.

Although the path towards professionalism has been a difficult one for many young players and the coaches who have worked with them, the hard work that Kraljević put in to nurture youth footballers in Singapore — some of whom he had personally coached and befriended over the years — has paid dividends. Using his contacts in Europe, Kraljević helped Singapore Youth Olympics star Bryan Neubronner secure a dream move of playing professional football with German club SSV Ulm 1846 in June 2013.[7] As the head coach of the Balestier S-League team, Kraljević gave the club's younger players a chance to play competitive football during his first full season as a top level coach — young players in Balestier's Prime League squad such as Nurullah Hussein, Hanafi Akbar and Ho Wai Loon were thrown straight into the senior team alongside the likes of Croats Goran Ljubojević and Emir Lotinac to help the club achieve a top-half finish and a well-deserved Singapore Cup title.

Kraljević is proud that the club has a positive attitude towards youth players. "Young Singapore players want to come to Balestier because they will get a chance to get playing experience, whereas the big clubs only want established or proven players," he says. In the 2015 season, these youth players will have even more playing opportunities as the club's Singapore Cup win has propelled them into the continental AFC Cup competition.[8] To Kraljević credit, the club's positive attitude towards aspiring youth players has much to do with the groundwork that he had put in to develop its youth setup over the space of a decade. Today, the club is only one in three in Singapore to have retained their Centre of Excellence, and their focus on youth meant that Balestier had one of the most youthful sides in the S-League in 2014 with only two players over the age of 30. This is no doubt a major achievement for a football club with limited financial resources, and with

---

[7] "Neubronner Relishing German Experience," *Axross The Line*, 25 February 2013. Retrieved 4 March 2015 from http://axrosstheline.com/2013/02/neubronner-relishing-german-experience.html.

[8] M. Yazid, "Balestier Looking to Put Up a Fight in AFC Cup," *VOXSPORTS*, 12 December 2014. Retrieved 4 March 2015 from http://voxsports.co/balestier-looking-to-put-up-a-fight-in-afc-cup.

much of the groundwork already laid by their hardworking and forward-looking Croatian legend, there may be more good things to look forward to for Balestier Khalsa fans in the years ahead.

Business, Futsal and the Future of Singapore Football

Kraljević's appetite for challenges goes beyond his coaching career — his other significant contribution to Singapore is the futsal company Stadio which he co-owns with his good friend V. Sundramoorthy. "The idea was developed while Sundram and I were at Jurong FC, and after someone we knew alerted us to this opportunity," Kraljević tells us. From a business point of view, the duo's investment gradually paid off because they correctly saw back then that Singaporeans wanted venues to play football games on a social rather than competitive basis. Over a decade later, Stadio is a successful sports company with 12 installations across six locations in Singapore, the latest being a futsal pitch placed on a rooftop at Tanjong Pagar's Amara Hotel.[9]

The increase in the number of futsal facilities and the safe environment in which futsal is played has helped to attract more health-conscious Singaporeans to take up futsal as a sporting activity. "Girls, old, young, students and people from all walks of life are all playing futsal now," he says proudly. Given the growing interest in futsal here, Kraljević often wonders why Singapore does not have a national futsal league yet! From a sporting point of view, as Kraljević tells us, futsal is a great game for learning technique and creativity because it requires its players to think fast thanks to the enclosed small pitch — similar to the conditions that he had experienced playing football on the streets of Osijek and those in Croatian schools today. In fact, Kraljević also capitalises on the unique developmental aspects of futsal by bringing his players down to Stadio to develop the technical parts of their game.

As an expert of the game who has called Singapore home for over two decades, Kraljević is also highly aware of the challenges that Singapore football faces. The debate on how Singapore's most popular sport can be improved continues to rage on in various quarters, and for Kraljević, he draws upon several policy ideas in Europe that Singapore can implement to improve football development here. One example relates to the use of Singapore's sports infrastructure for youth development — Kraljević correctly notes that Singapore's infrastructure of artificial football pitches in schools is among the best in the world and children and teenagers should be allowed to make full use of these facilities to further develop a strong football culture here. Adding on to that, Kraljević feels that schools should also

---

[9] A. Khan, "Amara Singapore Opens First Hotel Futsal Pitch," *Goal.com*., 7 March 2014. Retrieved 4 March 2015 from http://www.goal.com/en-sg/news/3880/singapore/2014/03/07/4666543/amara-singapore-opens-rooftop-futsal-pitch.

help young footballers develop their technical and creative skills on futsal pitches and not on large football pitches, as the development of such skills improves when young players are forced to think and play fast.

The system for youth development is another area that needs to be nurtured in Singapore. Kraljević also sees the need for Singapore football to professionalise its youth programs outside of the S-League level, in particular, the amateur National Football League (NFL) competition behind the professional S-League. "The NFL simply needs to get better in line with the S-League season," he says. "Every club from the S-League downwards must have youth development in order to develop more competitive players." His views echo those of far-sighted reformers of the game in EU member states such as Germany and Belgium, where a nationwide overhaul of youth development was implemented after disastrous performances by their national teams at international tournaments in the early 2000s.[10,11] Such reforms have already paid dividends as the Belgian and German teams lit up 2014 FIFA World Cup with their attacking play, with the latter nation securing the World Cup trophy for the fourth time in its history.

Last but not least, Kraljević has a dream that football clubs here will become strong community institutions like the clubs in Europe. This is all the more important in a country where there are more supporters of Manchester United and Arsenal than those of local clubs such as Balestier Khalsa and Geylang International. Community work is crucial for clubs anywhere in the world to develop a close bond to the people who live near the clubs' home grounds, Kraljević feels, and football fixtures — both youth and senior — should be played at times where families would be able to give their support to football clubs. Here, he mentions the example of UEFA's decision to switch the European Champions League final match day to a Saturday instead of the traditional Wednesday, citing President Michel Platini's wish that more families and children could catch the game if played over the weekend.[12]

Although the circumstances here are markedly different from those in Europe, the evidence from abroad suggests that the changes that Kraljević dreams about are not impossible. At a forum held in December 2014, the Football Association of Singapore's youth development head affirmed the importance of youth development in Singapore by stressing that plans are being put in place for clubs to work closely with Singapore's Ministry of Education and schools to try to cater to the

---

[10] S. James, "How Germany Went from Bust to Boom on the Talent Production Line," *The Guardian*, 23 May 2013. Retrieved 4 March 2015 from http://www.theguardian.com/football/2013/may/23/germany-bust-boom-talent.

[11] S. James, "Belgium's Blueprint that Gave Birth to a Golden Generation," *The Guardian*, 6 June 2014. Retrieved 4 March 2015 from http://www.theguardian.com/football/blog/2014/jun/06/belgium-blueprint-gave-birth-golden-generation-world-cup-.

[12] "Champions League Final Switched," *BBC Sport*, 30 November 2007. Retrieved 4 March 2015 from http://news.bbc.co.uk/sport2/hi/football/europe/7120518.stm.

best interests of these young aspiring footballers.[13] Also, Singapore's Ministry of Education and the Ministry of Community, Culture and Youth (MCCY) announced shortly after this interview that they are opening sports facilities in every school to encourage Singaporeans to take up sports.[14] Although these plans may only be the first steps in a long journey, they are nevertheless ones that create opportunities for Singapore football to evolve in the manner Kraljević has envisioned.

Calling Singapore "Home"

Having lived for nearly two decades in Singapore, what does Kraljević think about settling down in Singapore? "I never really thought about settling down in Asia. Usually football players think of making money and then going back home, but step by step I settled down here, got married and had kids." Kraljević is married to a Singaporean and has two children who attend public schools here. After 23 years in Singapore, he has fallen in love with pretty much everything about Singapore, including a unique aspect of the Lion City that many Singaporeans are proud to talk about. "I pretty much like all the local food here. Chicken rice is my favourite, Indian food as well especially when Sundram asks me for dinner, and also *kopi* (local coffee)."

Of course, Kraljević still keeps in close contact with his family back home in Osijek and he goes back home often, but back in Croatia is where he is often in high praise of Singapore. Speaking of his trips back home, he happily noted that he often meets many Singaporean students in Croatia on holiday — a testament to Singapore's standing in Asia where its citizens have the strong financial ability to venture beyond Singapore's shores. He also has much praise for Singapore's multi-racial society and spectacular economic development that has won it fans even in Croatia. "What Singapore has achieved since 1965 is amazing, you know. Even politicians back home are always talking about how we can be like Singapore."

But for now, working and doing business in Singapore is something he truly enjoys, and life here has been good to him. "My passport says I'm Croatian but I feel like I'm Singaporean now. I enjoy watching my children grow up here," he says. Also, Balestier Khalsa can almost be considered his second family in Singapore: As he tells us, he is very happy to be at the club with many familiar faces, including the kit man who has been there since his playing days!

---

[13] N. Chin, "Mentality and System Fault Present Challenges for FAS in Developing Youths," *Yahoo Sports Singapore*, 2 December 2014. Retrieved 4 March 2015 from https://sg.sports.yahoo.com/news/mentality-system-fault-present-challenges-fas-developing-youths-174200638--spt.html.

[14] I. De Cotta, "Sports Facilities in Every School to be Opened to the Public: Lawrence Wong," *TODAY*, 20 January 2015. Retrieved 4 March 2015 from http://www.todayonline.com/sports/sports-facilities-every-school-be-opened-public-lawrence-wong.

As is the case with local football stars such as Daniel Bennett and Aleksandar Đurić, Singapore is where Kraljević firmly calls home now. Here is where he intends to be in his long term and he does not plan on moving back to his homeland anytime soon — certainly, this is good news for Balestier Khalsa and fans of Singapore football. When asked about what he felt was his proudest moment in Singapore, Kraljević smiles and answers "Not yet." Stay tuned, Singapore: there is plenty to look forward to more from this dynamic individual who has yet more dreams to fulfil here.

Dexter Lee is Programme and Policy Executive at the EU Centre.

World Scientific Series on Singapore's 50 Years of Nation-Building

Forthcoming (continued from page ii)

50 Years of Materials Science
   edited by Freddy Boey (Nanyang Technological University, Singapore), Subramanian Lakshmi Venkatraman (Nanyang Technological University, Singapore) and B.V.R. Chowdari (National University of Singapore, Singapore)

50 Years of Real Estate in Singapore
   edited by Deng Yongheng, Seek Ngee Huat, Sing Tien Foo and Yu Shi-Ming (National University of Singapore, Singapore)

The Singapore Research Story
   *edited by Hang Chang Chieh (National University of Singapore, Singapore), Low Teck Seng (National Research Foundation, Singapore) and Raj Thampuran (A*Star, Singapore)*

50 Years of Science
   edited by Lim Hock (National University of Singapore, Singapore), Bernard Tan (National University of Singapore, Singapore) and K.K. Phua (World Scientific Publishing Company, Singapore, and Imperial College Press, London)

Perspectives on the Security of Singapore: The First 50 Years
   edited by Barry Desker and Ang Cheng Guan (S. Rajaratnam School of International Studies, Nanyang Technological University, Singapore)

Singapore–China Relations: 50 Years
   edited by Zheng Yongnian and Lye Liang Fook (East Asian Institute, National University of Singapore, Singapore)

50 Years of Singapore and the United Nations
   edited by Tommy Koh (Ambassador-at-Large, Singapore), Chang Li Lin (Prime Minister's Office, Singapore) and Joanna Koh (Institute of Policy Studies, Singapore)

50 Years of Technical Education in Singapore: How to Build a World Class Education System from Scratch
   by N. Varaprasad (Partner and Principal Consultant, Singapore Education Consulting Group, and founding Principal and CEO, Temasek Polytechnic)

50 Years of Transportation in Singapore: Achievements and Challenges
   edited by Fwa Tien Fang (National University of Singapore, Singapore)

50 Years of Urban Planning in Singapore
   edited by Heng Chye Kiang (National University of Singapore, Singapore)